SASKA  N
MANITOBA
NATURE
GUIDE

Krista Kagume
with contributions from
Jim McCormac

Lone Pine Publishing

Distributed by: Canada Book Distributors - Booklogic
www.canadabookdistributors.com
www.lonepinepublishing.com
Tel: 1-800-661-9017

Canadian Cataloguing in Publication Data

Kagume, Krista
  Saskatchewan and Manitoba nature guide / Krista Kagume.

Includes bibliographical references and index.
ISBN 78-1-77451-049-0

  1. Natural history--Saskatchewan--Guidebooks. 2. Natural history--Manitoba--Guidebooks. I. Title.

QH106.2.S38K34 2020   578.097124   C2010-900374-

Editorial Director: Nancy Foulds
Editor: Wendy Pirk, Sheila Quinlan
Production Manager: Gene Longson
Designer: Heather Markham
Layout: Volker Bodegom, Rob Tao
Cover Design: Gerry Dotto
Cover Images: Frank Burman, Linda Dunn, Ted Nordhagen, Gary Ross, Ian Sheldon
Illustrations Credits: see p. 4

Disclaimer: This guide is not intended to be a "how to" reference guide for food or medicinal uses of plants. We do not recommend experimentation by readers, and we caution that a number of plants in Saskatchewan and Manitoba, including some used traditionally as medicines, are poisonous and harmful.

We acknowledge the financial support of the Government of Canada.
Nous reconnaissons l'appui financier du gouvernement du Canada.

Funded by the Government of Canada
Financé par le gouvernement du Canada | Canadä

PC: 38-1

TABLE OF CONTENTS

ILLUSTRATION CREDITS

Charity Briere 134a, 135a, 137b

Frank Burman 132ab, 152b, 154b, 155abcd, 156a, 157cd, 158ab, 159b, 160c, 162b, 163abc, 164a, 165d, 166cd, 169ab, 170a, 171bc, 172abc, 173abc, 174c, 175abc, 176ab, 177ac, 179ab, 180b, 181ab, 182abc, 183bc, 184ab, 185c, 186ac, 187abc, 188a, 189b, 190a, 191bc, 193ac, 194ab, 195abc, 196a, 197a, 198bc, 199abc, 200bc, 201abc, 202abc

Ivan Droujinin 140bc

Linda Dunn 169c, 188b, 200a

Kindrie Grove 59b, 75abc

Linda Kershaw 151b

Ted Nordhagen 87c, 88bc, 89a, 90ab, 91c, 93c, 96b, 98abc, 99ab, 102a, 103bc, 104bc, 105ab, 107ac, 109ac, 110ac, 111abc

George Penetrante 126a, 127c, 129ab, 135b

Ewa Pluciennik 97b

Gary Ross 48b, 50ab, 51ab, 52ab, 53ab, 54ab, 55abc, 56abc, 57abc, 58abc, 59a, 60ab, 61abc, 62abc, 63abc, 64abc, 65ab, 66abc, 67ab, 68ab, 69abc, 70abc, 71ab, 72ab, 73ab, 74abc, 78ab, 79ab, 80abc, 81abc, 82abc, 83abc, 84ab, 85ab, 86abc, 87ab, 88a, 89bc, 90c, 91ab, 92abc, 93ab, 94ab, 95ab, 96ac, 97ac, 99c, 100ab, 101ab, 102bc, 103a, 104a, 105c, 106abc, 107b, 108abc, 109b, 110b, 113abc, 114abc, 115abc, 116ab, 117ab, 118ab, 119ab, 120ab

Ian Sheldon 48a, 49ab, 123abc, 124abc, 125abc, 126bc, 127ab, 128abc, 129c, 130abc, 133ab, 134b, 136abc, 137ac, 138abc, 139abc, 140a, 141abc, 142abc, 143abc, 146abc, 147abc, 148abcde, 149abcdef, 150abcde, 151acde, 152ac, 154a, 156b, 157ab, 158c, 159a, 160ab, 161abcd, 162ac, 164bc, 165abc, 166ab, 170bc, 171a, 174ab, 176c, 177b, 178abc, 179c, 180ac, 181c, 183a, 184c, 185ab, 186b, 188c, 189ac, 190bc, 191a, 192abc, 193b, 194c, 196bc, 197bc, 198a

ACKNOWLEDGEMENTS

The publisher and author would like to thank the many authors of former Lone Pine texts who have created such a great library of background information, as well as the talented illustrators, editorial and production staff.

Special thanks to: Norm Kenkel of the University of Manitoba Biology Department, for his suggestions and comments on plant species; Robert Sission, Grasslands National Park Biologist, for providing the latest black-tailed prairie dog and Ord's kangaroo rat status reports; and also to Ian Stirling for comments on marine animals.

MAMMALS

Beluga
p. 48

Harbour Seal
p. 48

Ringed Seal
p. 49

Bearded Seal
p. 49

Bison
p. 50

North American Elk
p. 50

White-tailed Deer
p. 51

Mule Deer
p. 51

Moose
p. 52

Caribou
p. 52

Pronghorn
p. 53

Cougar
p. 53

Canada Lynx
p. 54

Bobcat
p. 54

Striped Skunk
p. 55

American Marten
p. 55

Fisher
p. 55

Least Weasel
p. 56

Short-tailed Weasel
p. 56

Long-tailed Weasel
p. 56

Mink
p. 57

Black-footed Ferret
p. 57

Wolverine
p. 57

Badger
p. 58

Northern River Otter
p. 58

Raccoon
p. 58

Black Bear
p. 59

Polar Bear
p. 59

Coyote
p. 60

Grey Wolf
p. 60

Arctic Fox
p. 61

Swift Fox
p. 61

Red Fox
p. 61

Porcupine
p. 62

Meadow Jumping Mouse
p. 62

Brown Rat
p. 62

MAMMALS

House Mouse
p. 63

Deer Mouse
p. 63

Meadow Vole
p. 63

Northern Bog Lemming
p. 64

Ord's Kangaroo Rat
p. 64

Olive-backed Pocket Mouse
p. 64

Muskrat
p. 65

Beaver
p. 65

Least Chipmunk
p. 66

Woodchuck
p. 66

Red Squirrel
p. 67

Eastern Grey Squirrel
p. 67

Fox Squirrel
p. 68

Northern Flying Squirrel
p. 68

Thirteen-lined Ground Squirrel
p. 69

Richardson's Ground Squirrel
p. 69

Black-tailed Prairie Dog
p. 69

Northern Pocket Gopher
p. 70

MAMMALS

Snowshoe Hare
p. 70

White-tailed Jackrabbit
p. 70

Nuttall's Cottontail
p. 71

Eastern Cottontail
p. 71

Northern Bat
p. 72

Little Brown Bat
p. 72

Red Bat
p. 73

Hoary Bat
p. 73

Silver-haired Bat
p. 74

Big Brown Bat
p. 74

Star-nosed Mole
p. 74

Masked Shrew
p. 75

Northern Water Shrew
p. 75

Pygmy Shrew
p. 75

BIRDS

Snow Goose
p. 78

Canada Goose
p. 78

Tundra Swan
p. 79

Wood Duck
p. 79

Mallard
p. 80

Blue-Winged Teal
p. 80

BIRDS

Northern Pintail
p. 80

Northern Shoveler
p. 81

Canvasback
p. 81

Lesser Scaup
p. 81

Common Goldeneye
p. 82

Common Merganser
p. 82

Ruddy Duck
p. 82

Gray Partridge
p. 83

Ruffed Grouse
p. 83

Sharp-tailed Grouse
p. 83

Common Loon
p. 84

Red-necked Grebe
p. 84

American White Pelican
p. 85

Double-crested Cormorant
p. 85

American Bittern
p. 86

Great Blue Heron
p. 86

Turkey Vulture
p. 86

Bald Eagle
p. 87

Northern Harrier
p. 87

Swainson's Hawk
p. 87

Red-tailed Hawk
p. 88

American Kestrel
p. 88

Merlin
p. 88

Sora
p. 89

American Coot
p. 89

Sandhill Crane
p. 89

Killdeer
p. 90

American Avocet
p. 90

Spotted Sandpiper
p. 90

Lesser Yellowlegs
p. 91

Wilson's Snipe
p. 91

Wilson's Phalarope
p. 91

Franklin's Gull
p. 92

Ring-billed Gull
p. 92

Common Tern
p. 92

Black Tern
p. 93

BIRDS

Rock Pigeon
p. 93

Mourning Dove
p. 93

Great Horned Owl
p. 94

Snowy Owl
p. 94

Short-eared Owl
p. 95

Burrowing Owl
p. 95

Common Nighthawk
p. 96

Ruby-throated Hummingbird
p. 96

Belted Kingfisher
p. 96

Downy Woodpecker
p. 97

Northern Flicker
p. 97

Pileated Woodpecker
p. 97

Least Flycatcher
p. 98

Eastern Phoebe
p. 98

Eastern Kingbird
p. 98

Northern Shrike
p. 99

Red-eyed Vireo
p. 99

Gray Jay
p. 99

Blue Jay
p. 100

Black-billed Magpie
p. 100

American Crow
p. 101

Common Raven
p. 101

Horned Lark
p. 102

Tree Swallow
p. 102

Barn Swallow
p. 102

Black-capped Chickadee
p. 103

Red-breasted Nuthatch
p. 103

House Wren
p. 103

Mountain Bluebird
p. 104

American Robin
p. 104

Gray Catbird
p. 104

Brown Thrasher
p. 105

European Starling
p. 105

Bohemian Waxwing
p. 105

Yellow Warbler
p. 106

Warbler Yellow-Rumped
p. 106

American Redstart
p. 106

Common Yellowthroat
p. 107

Spotted Towhee
p. 107

Chipping Sparrow
p. 107

White-throated Sparrow
p. 108

Dark-eyed Junco
108

Rose-breasted Grosbeak
p. 108

BIRDS

Red-Winged Blackbird
p. 109

Western Meadowlark
p. 109

Yellow-headed Blackbird
p. 109

Brown-headed Cowbird
p. 110

Baltimore Oriole
p. 110

Purple Finch
p. 110

Common Redpoll
p. 111

American Goldfinch
p. 111

House Sparrow
p. 111

AMPHIBIANS & REPTILES

Mudpuppy
p. 113

Blue-spotted Salamander
p. 113

Tiger Salamander
p. 113

Plains Spadefoot Toad
p. 114

American Toad
p. 114

Canadian Toad
p. 114

Grey Treefrog
p. 115

Spring Peeper
p. 115

Boreal Chorus Frog
p. 115

Northern Leopard Frog
p. 116

Wood Frog
p. 116

AMPHIBIANS & REPTILES

Common Snapping Turtle
p. 117

Western Painted Turtle
p. 117

Greater Short-horned Lizard
p. 118

Smooth Greensnake
p. 118

Red-bellied Snake
p. 119

Red-sided Gartersnake
p. 119

Western Hog-nosed Snake
p. 120

Prairie Rattlesnake
p. 120

FISH

Lake Sturgeon
p. 123

Rainbow Trout
p. 123

Brown Trout
p. 123

Brook Trout
p. 124

Lake Trout
p. 124

Lake Whitefish
p. 124

Arctic Grayling
p. 125

Goldeye
p. 125

Northern Pike
p. 125

Common Carp
p. 126

Emerald Shiner
p. 126

Longnose Sucker
p. 126

FISH

White Sucker
p. 127

Black Bullhead
p. 127

Channel Catfish
p. 127

Burbot
p. 128

Brook Stickleback
p. 128

Trout-perch
p. 128

Rock Bass
p. 129

Smallmouth Bass
p. 129

Yellow Perch
p. 129

Walleye
p. 130

Iowa Darter
p. 130

Slimy Sculpin
p. 130

INVERTEBRATES

Cabbage White
p. 132

Canadian Tiger Swallowtail
p. 132

Spring Azure
p. 133

Mourning Cloak
p. 133

Monarch
p. 134

Polyphemus Moth
p. 134

Woolly Bear Caterpillar
p. 135

Tent Caterpillar
p. 135

Multicoloured Asian Ladybug
p. 136

Spruce Sawyer
p. 136

Crane Flies
p. 136

Carpenter Ant
p. 137

Bumblebee
p. 137

Yellow Jacket
p. 137

Green Stink Bug
p. 138

Green Lacewing
p. 138

Road Duster Grasshopper
p. 138

Boreal Bluet
p. 139

Green Darner
p. 139

Cherry-faced Meadowhawk
p. 139

Mayfly
p. 140

Virile Crayfish
p. 140

Water Strider
p. 140

Caddisfly Larvae
p. 141

Water Boatman
p. 141

Giant Diving Beetle
p. 141

Fishing Spider
p. 142

Orbweavers
p. 142

Harvestmen
p. 142

Garden Centipedes
p. 143

Sowbug
p. 143

Northern Scorpion
p. 143

TREES & TALL SHRUBS

Balsam Fir
p. 146

White Spruce
p. 146

Black Spruce
p. 146

Tamarack
p. 147

Jack Pine
p. 147

White Elm
p. 147

Bur Oak
p. 148

Paper Birch
p. 148

Water Birch
p. 148

Speckled Alder
p. 149

Trembling Aspen
p. 149

Eastern Cottonwood
p. 149

Balsam Poplar
p. 150

Pin Cherry
p. 150

Choke Cherry
p. 150

Showy Mountain-ash
p. 151

Hawthorns
p. 151

Saskatoon
p. 151

Mountain Maple
p. 151

Manitoba Maple
p. 152

Green Ash
p. 152

Common Juniper
p. 154

Crowberry
p. 154

Dwarf Birch
p. 155

Beaked Hazelnut
p. 155

Sweet Gale
p. 156

Pussy Willow
p. 156

Red-osier Dogwood
p. 157

Alder-leaved Buckthorn
p. 157

Cloudberry
p. 157

Wild Red Raspberry
p. 158

Prickly Wild Rose
p. 158

Shrubby Cinquefoil
p. 159

Narrow-leaved Meadowsweet
p. 159

Bristly Black Currant
p. 160

Skunk Currant
p. 160

Canada Buffaloberry
p. 161

Wolf Willow
p. 161

Silver Sagebrush
p. 161

Common Rabbitbrush
p. 162

Labrador Tea
p. 162

Bearberry
p. 162

SHRUBS & VINES

Velvet Leaf Blueberry
p. 163

Lingonberry
p. 163

Leatherleaf
p. 163

Dwarf Bog Rosemary
p. 164

Prince's Pine
p. 164

Twinflower
p. 164

Common Snowberry
p. 165

Nannyberry
p. 165

Highbrush
p. 165

Bracted Honeysuckle
p. 166

White Clematis
p. 166

Poison Ivy
p. 166

FORBS, FERNS & GRASSES

Yellow Lady's-slipper
p. 169

Common Blue-eyed-Grass
p. 169

Wood Lily
p. 169

Wild Lily-of-the-valley
p. 170

Starry False Solomon's-seal
p. 170

Prairie Onion
p. 170

White Death-camas
p. 171

Yellow Umbrellaplant
p. 171

Western Dock
p. 171

Stinging Nettle
p. 172

Strawberry Blite
p. 172

Red Saltwort
p. 172

Prairie Crocus
p. 173

Canada Anemone
p. 173

Yellow Marsh-marigold
p. 173

Meadow Buttercup
p. 174

Red Baneberry
p. 174

Wild Columbine
p. 174

Meadowrue
p. 175

Beeplant
p. 175

Round-leaf Sundew
p. 175

Pitcher-plant
p. 176

Grass-of-Parnassus
p. 176

Virginia Strawberry
p. 176

Common Silverweed
p. 177

Three-flowered Avens
p. 177

Purple Prairie-clover
p. 177

Alfalfa
p. 178

Sweet-clover
p. 178

Showy Locoweed
p. 178

FORBS, FERNS & GRASSES

American Licorice
p. 179

Golden-bean
p. 179

Red Clover
p. 179

American Vetch
p. 180

Northern Crane's-bill
p. 180

Flax
p. 180

Spotted Touch-me-not
p. 181

Leafy Spurge
p. 181

Scarlet Globemallow
p. 181

Canada Violet
p. 182

Pincushion Cactus
p. 182

Prickly-pear Cactus
p. 182

Common Fireweed
p. 183

Scarlet Beeblossom
p. 183

Common Evening-primrose
p. 183

Wild Sarsaparilla
p. 184

Spotted Water-hemlock
p. 184

Common Cow-parsnip
p. 184

Bunchberry
p. 185

Common Pink Wintergreen
p. 185

Saline Shootingstar
p. 185

Fringed Loosestrife
p. 186

Spreading Dogbane
p. 186

Showy Milkweed
p. 186

Narrow-leaved Puccoon
p. 187

Tall Bluebells
p. 187

Blue Giant-hyssop
p. 187

Wild Mint
p. 188

Wild Bergamot
p. 188

Common Red Paintbrush
p. 188

Butter-and-eggs
p. 189

False-toadflax
p. 189

Northern Bedstraw
p. 189

Bluets
p. 190

Harebell
p. 190

Common Yarrow
p. 190

Pussytoes
p. 191

Common Burdock
p. 191

Nodding Beggar's-ticks
p. 191

Canada Thistle
p. 192

Great Blanketflower
p. 192

Curly-cup Gumweed
p. 192

Common Sunflower
p. 193

Narrow-leaved Hawkweed
p. 193

Common Blue Lettuce
p. 193

Oxeye Daisy
p. 194

Dotted Blazingstar
p. 194

Pineapple-weed
p. 194

FORBS, FERNS & GRASSES

Coltsfoot
p. 195

Prairie Coneflower
p. 195

Black-eyed Susan
p. 195

Marsh Ragwort
p. 196

Canada Goldenrod
p. 196

Perennial Sow-thistle
p. 196

Fringed Aster
p. 197

Common Tansy
p. 197

Common Dandelion
p. 197

Common Goat's-beard
p. 198

Ostrich Fern
p. 198

Common Horsetail
p. 198

Buck-bean
p. 199

Arum-leaved Arrowhead
p. 199

Thread-leaved Watercrowfoot
p. 199

Yellow Pond-lily
p. 200

Water Calla
p. 200

Water Smartweed
p. 200

Common Bladderwort
p. 201

Common Cattail
p. 201

Big Bluestem
p. 201

Blue Grama Grass
p. 202

Needle-and-thread Grass
p. 202

Foxtail Barley
p. 202

INTRODUCTION

The natural regions of Saskatchewan and Manitoba are well appreciated by both residents and visitors. These central Canadian provinces are as diverse as they are large, stretching from the agricultural plains and parklands of the south, through the rich boreal forest, the lakes and rivers of the subarctic, to the rugged Hudson Bay coastline of northern Manitoba. Foresight in establishing protected areas and provincial and national parks has conserved areas of wilderness for us to experience and appreciate. Even beyond protected borders, parts of Saskatchewan and Manitoba are still wild enough for foxes, bears and hawks, and remote enough for elusive species such as wolverine and wolves. Our own backyards host bold, opportunistic species such as coyotes, deer and many birds, insects and rodents. We can view magnificent polar bears in Churchill, Manitoba, enjoy trophy fishing in our northern lakes, celebrate an extensive assemblage of breeding birds in the boreal forest and marvel at rattlesnakes or scorpions in Saskatchewan's southwestern badlands.

This guide provides an overview of the incredible diversity of Saskatchewan and Manitoba, but it is just a beginning. Thousands of animals and plants occur here, enough to fill several volumes. We hope this book helps you discover the rich natural history of our region.

Grey Wolf

THE REGIONS

Southern Arctic

Caribou

Characterized by short, cool summers, long, cold winters and low precipitation, the Southern Arctic runs through the Northwest Territories and northern Quebec, dipping into the extreme northeast corner of Manitoba along Hudson Bay. The southern edge of this ecozone is marked by the treeline, north of which there are no full-sized trees. Low, stunted trees, small shrubs, lichen and sedges (*Carex* spp.) are some characteristic plants found here. Larger animals include polar bears, caribou and wolves. Smaller lemmings, shrews and voles are prey for weasels, wolverines and foxes. Birds migrate and nest here, but few remain through the harsh winter, and the climate is too cold for reptiles and amphibians. Few humans live here, with human activities including hunting, trapping, fishing, natural resource exploration and extraction, as well as tourism.

Hudson Plains

The Hudson Plains hug the southern shores of Hudson Bay and stretch from northern Manitoba to Quebec. Flat terrain and poor drainage combine to create the largest continuous wetlands in the world. The Hudson Plains are well known for their mosquito, blackfly and no-see-um populations; one hectare can produce up to 10 million biting insects!

Tamarack

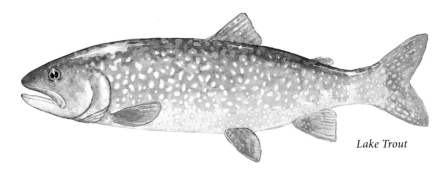

Lake Trout

Plant life includes treeless tundra to the north and taiga to the south, with characteristic trees such as black spruce, white spruce, tamarack, balsam poplar, dwarf birch and willow. Large carnivores such as polar bears, lynx and wolves are found here as well as the arctic fox, red fox and wolverine. Hudson Bay is home to seals and beluga whales. Bird diversity is highest in summer, when migrants come here to nest. Amphibians include wood frogs and boreal chorus frogs; fish include lake trout, sturgeon and walleye.

Taiga Shield

This ecozone represents the transition between arctic tundra and boreal forest. If you ever get the opportunity to fly over this part of the region, you will notice that it is densely dotted with lakes that run parallel along a northeast to southwest axis—a result of glaciation. Vegetation is limited to species that can tolerate harsh winter temperatures and a short growing season. The predominant forest type is classified as "lichen woodland" and is typified by open-canopy black spruce stands carpeted with lichen. Bogs and fens are found in lowland areas.

Only 0.1% of the region's population is found in this ecozone, and mining is the only major economic activity. As a result, wildlife habitat is less fragmented than in southern areas.

Because of the low diversity of vegetation and the difficult living conditions, wildlife diversity is also low. Caribou, wolves, black bears, lynx, otters and other smaller predators and herbivores live here.

Bohemian Waxwing

Approximately 120 bird species have been recorded, including nesting bohemian waxwings, dark-eyed juncos and lesser yellowlegs. Gray jays and common redpolls are year-round residents. Wood frogs and boreal chorus frogs may be found here, but there are no reptiles.

27

Boreal Shield

The Boreal Shield covers approximately one-third of the region and is associated with the Precambrian Shield. It is composed of broad, rolling, rough-surfaced uplands and lowlands. As in the Taiga Shield ecozone, the dominant tree species is black spruce, but forests in the Boreal Shield are often closed (with the crowns

Boreal Chorus Frog

of the trees touching) and the ground is usually carpeted with feather mosses. Upland forests often include fire-adapted jack pine, while moister, lowland forests include tamarack. Lakes and rivers are common and, as in the Taiga Shield ecozone, are arranged along a northeast to southwest axis. More diverse forest stands may be found around these water bodies. Wetland areas are also common, usually in the form of bogs or, less frequently, fens. This ecozone also includes the Athabasca sand dunes on the southern shore of Lake Athabasca, Saskatchewan, which contain plant species that cannot be found anywhere else in the world.

Less than 1% of the population lives here, but only a fragment of the land in this ecozone is protected in parks, such as Lac La Ronge Provincial Park, Saskatchewan. The main economic activities are mining and forestry.

Deer, moose, black bears, beavers, weasels, hares and red squirrels are some of the animals that occur here. The diversity of bird species in this ecozone is considered moderately low, with around 220 species reported. Gartersnakes, wood frogs, chorus frogs, spring peepers and American toads occur here; fish include lake trout, brook trout, lake whitefish and northern pike.

Northern Pike

Boreal Plain

Occupying approximately one-quarter of the region, the Boreal Plain ecozone lies between the southern edge of the Precambrian Shield and the Aspen Parkland ecoregion of the Prairie ecozone. The vegetation in this part of the region is diverse, owing to a relatively warm, humid climate. Closed-crown coniferous and mixed forests are characteristic, with the predominant coniferous species being white and black spruce, jack pine and tamarack, and the predominant deciduous species being aspen, paper birch and balsam poplar. Lakes and rivers are common, but they do not necessarily run in a northeast to southwest orientation as they do in more northern parts of the province. Wetlands are primarily in the form of fens, though bogs are present as well.

This ecozone supports approximately 15% of our population, and the main economic activities are forestry, agriculture, mining and oil and gas exploration.

The boreal plain supports a high diversity of species—from larger black bears, moose, lynx and deer to smaller porcupines, squirrels and chipmunks. Approximately 300 bird species have been recorded here. Fish include lake trout, brown trout, pike and walleye; amphibians and reptiles include wood frogs, mink frogs, chorus frogs, American toads and gartersnakes.

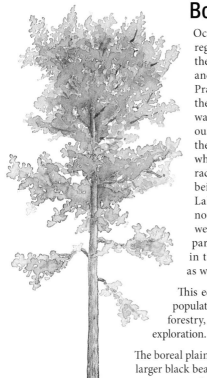

Balsam Poplar

Mixed Wood Shield

The Mixed Wood Shield in southeastern Manitoba is an extension of eastern mixedwood forests of the northern Great Lakes-St. Lawrence area, where limestone is the underlying rock. Eastern white cedar (*Thuja occidentalis*), eastern white pine (*Pinus strobus*), black ash (*Fraxinus nigra*), basswood (*Tilia americana*) and yellow birch (*Betula alleghaniensis*) reach the northernmost extension of their range here but occur nowhere else in Manitoba or Saskatchewan. The Mixed Wood Shield includes Lake of the Woods and Whiteshell Provincial Park, which preserves 2729 km² of natural area and allows for various nature-oriented leisure activities such as canoeing, cross-country skiing and fishing.

Caddisfly Larva

Prairie and Aspen Parkland

The Prairie ecozone covers the southern third of Saskatchewan and southwestern Manitoba. The Aspen Parkland ecoregion, a mosaic of fescue prairie and aspen forest, forms a belt across the northern portion of the temperate prairie and represents the transition between boreal forest and grasslands habitats. Much of the rest of the Prairie is made up of arid mixed-grass prairie including blue grama grass and other grasses, sedges and herbs. In more humid parts of the grasslands, wetlands are primarily fresh water, are more permanent and are bordered with willows and aspen. In the drier, southern parts, wetlands are impermanent and saline, resulting in shorelines with salt rings and little or no vegetation. The Cypress Upland ecoregion, in the southwest corner of Saskatchewan, rises high above the prairie. It is the only part of the province that escaped glaciation and is characterized by fescue prairie interspersed with forests composed primarily of lodgepole pine *(Pinus contorta)*, white spruce and aspen.

Blue Grama Grass

The Prairie ecozone contains the majority of the human population in Saskatchewan and Manitoba and is heavily fragmented. More than 80% of the native prairie landscape has been transformed by agriculture and urbanization. Many species that are heavily dependent upon native prairie, such as the prairie rattlesnake and the burrowing owl, are threatened or endangered. Parks and protected areas, including Grasslands National Park and Cypress Hills Provincial Park make up only 9% of the ecozone.

Large prairie animals include white-tailed deer, mule deer and pronghorn antelope. Coyotes, foxes, ground squirrels, northern pocket gophers, least chipmunks and beavers are also found here. During the summer breeding season, characteristic

Northern Pocket Gopher

Northern Scorpion

grasslands birds include western meadowlarks, horned larks, bluebirds, night-hawks and loggerhead shrikes; wetlands abound with waterfowl and shorebirds, and Swainson's hawks survey the landscape from the sky. Warmer water fish, such as pike, carp and yellow perch, occur in prairie lakes. Most of our amphibians and reptiles are found here, including frogs, toads, salamanders, snakes, turtles and one lizard. The dry grasslands of southwestern Saskatchewan house a number of rare species including the Ord's kangaroo rat and one species of scorpion; others such as the plains bison and black-footed ferret have been extirpated.

CHALLENGES

Conserving Manitoba and Saskatchewan's ecoregions and protecting their globally significant biodiversity is fraught with challenges. Human development, agriculture, mining, forestry and other human activities have obliterated or degraded many habitats. Streams and rivers carry pollutants to Hudson Bay. Invasive non-native animal and plant species such as European starlings and leafy spurge have taken hold and reduced native biodiversity. In spite of those adversities, the Prairie Provinces remain a bastion of diversity, ranging from the scorpions of southwestern Saskatchewan to the polar bears of northern Manitoba, with many more common species found in between. We hope this guide helps introduce more people to the wonders of Saskatchewan and Manitoba and encourages visitors to tread lightly in our wild places.

Leafy Spurge

31

SELECT SASKATCHEWAN WILDLIFE WATCHING SITES

Saskatchewan is as diverse as it is large, from the relatively untouched, subarctic forests with their dense network of lakes and rivers, or the lush central boreal forests with rich flora and fauna, to the arid southern prairie with scattered saline wetlands. Because of this diversity, it has a lot to offer wildlife species (and humans!). In fact, the Boreal Plain ecoregion of Saskatchewan, Alberta and Manitoba has the distinction of having Canada's most extensive assemblage of breeding birds.

There are hundreds of good wilderness areas throughout the province. The following areas have been selected to represent a broad range of habitats, with an emphasis on diversity and accessibility.

Canadian Tiger Swallowtail

BOREAL SHIELD

1. Lac La Ronge PP

BOREAL PLAIN

2. Besnard Lake
3. Candle Lake PP
4. Clarence-Steepbank Lakes PP
5. Duck Mountain PP
6. Greenwater Lake PP
7. Hudson Bay
8. Makwa Lake PP
9. Meadow Lake PP
10. Narrow Hills PP
11. Nisbet PF
12. Prince Albert NP
13. Tobin Lake

PRAIRIE

14. Blackstrap Reservoir/PP
15. Buffalo Pound PP and Nicolle Flats
16. Buffer Lake
17. Chaplin Lake/Marsh
18. Crooked Lake PP
19. Cypress Hills PP
20. Danielson PP and Gardiner Dam
21. Douglas PP
22. Eastend
23. Echo Valley PP
24. Estevan
25. Foam Lake Marsh
26. Good Spirit Lake PP
27. Grasslands NP
28. Katepwa Point PP
29. Kindersley
30. Last Mountain Lake NWA
31. Leader
32. Luck Lake
33. Maple Creek
34. Moose Mountain PP
35. Pike Lake PP
36. Ponass Lake
37. Quill Lakes
38. Radisson Lake
39. Redberry Lake
40. Regina Beach
41. Saskatchewan Landing PP

NWA = National Wildlife Area
NP = National Park
PF = Provincial Forest
PP = Provincial Park

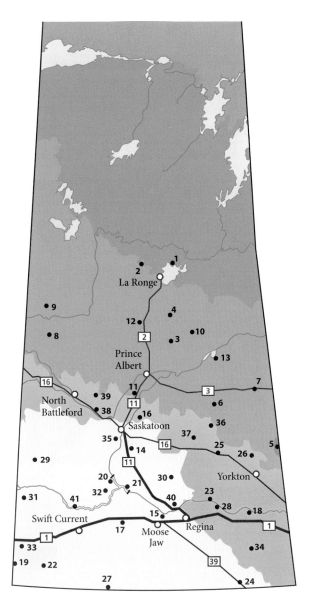

Saskatchewan

- Taiga Shield
- Boreal Shield
- Boreal Plains
- Aspen Parkland
- Mixed Grass Prairie
- Cypress Upland

Beaver Creek Conservation Area

Located 13 km south of Saskatoon, this natural area protects native short-grass prairie and a sheltered river valley. The interpretive centre focuses on discovering nature, cultural heritage and the health of the Saskatchewan River Basin. Five nature trails provide excellent wildlife watching or birdwatching and may lead to glimpses of coyotes, catbirds or hawks.

Buffalo Pound Provincial Park

Buffalo Pound Provincial Park is west of Regina in the Qu'Appelle Valley—an oasis of rolling hills, lakes and unique flora and fauna. The park is on the south-eastern end of Buffalo Pound Lake, a 35-km long reservoir popular for its walleye and pike. Nicolle Flats Interpretive Area is found in the southeast corner of the park and has several walking trails, a boardwalk through the marsh and interpretive services. Expect to find birds, plants, insects and other wetland animals. Captive bison, occupying a pasture near the interpretive area, can be seen from the Bison View Trail and observation tower.

Red-tailed Hawk

Bison

Burrowing Owl Interpretive Centre

This educational centre in Moose Jaw offers insight into the ecology of one of our region's endangered species. The centre focuses on conserving burrowing owls and their native prairie habitat. It is located on the Moose Jaw Exhibition Grounds, where several pairs of burrowing owls nest.

Chaplin Nature Centre

The Chaplin Nature Centre is conveniently located right on the TransCanada Highway in southern Saskatchewan and provides information on migratory birds, brine shrimp and other prey, as well as local history and agricultural practices. Hundreds of thousands of birds pass through Chaplin Lake during spring and autumn migration, while scores of others nest here.

Burrowing Owl

The area is known for its migrating shore-birds—up to 50,000 sanderlings (*Calidris alba*) have been counted in one day here—but endangered species such as burrowing owls may also be sighted in the area. Chaplin supports more than 30 species of shorebirds, many of which can be seen from observation towers. Chaplin is one of only two Western Hemispheric Shorebird Reserve Network sites in Canada, signifying hemispheric importance.

Wilson's Snipe

CYPRESS HILLS

The lodgepole pine forests of Cypress Hills rise out of the floodplains in southwestern Saskatchewan like a displaced boreal foothill lost in a sea of grass. Wildlife typically found in the Rocky Mountains or boreal forests, such as moose, elk, deer and cougar, find themselves isolated in these hills. Birdwatchers will enjoy more than 200 species, including mountain species such as the pink-sided variation of the dark-eyed junco or the "Audubon's" yellow-rumped warbler and boreal species such as the ruffed grouse. Grassland animals include mule deer and northern leopard frogs and wild turkeys (*Meleagris gallopavo*). Plant life not found elsewhere in the prairies abounds here, including yellow lady's-slipper and 13 other orchid species.

Yellow Lady's-slipper

GRASSLANDS NATIONAL PARK

Grasslands National Park protects 200 km^2 of rolling prairie grasslands, one of Canada's most endangered habitats. The park is made up of two separate blocks: the west block is on the Frenchman River Valley; the east block contains the Killdeer "Badlands" and Wood Mountain "Uplands." Settlement and agricultural development have resulted in the extirpation of bison, black-footed ferret, swift fox and other grassland species, but many others have found refuge in and around Grasslands National Park. The distinctive blend of both common and endangered species includes the pronghorn, peregrine falcon, burrowing owl, prairie rattlesnake and short-horned lizard. Plant species include prickly pear cactus, blue grama brass, sagebrush and evening-primrose.

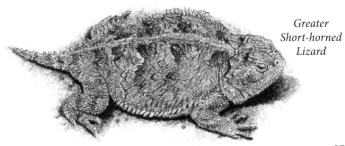

Greater Short-horned Lizard

Lake Diefenbaker

Lake Diefenbaker, Saskatchewan's largest freshwater lake, is often referred to as the "jewel of the prairies." This man-made lake is home to 27 fish species and attracts many animals, from the great blue heron and double-crested cormorant to the endangered piping plover (*Charadrius melodus*). Sharp-tailed grouse, mule deer and white-tailed deer are found in the surrounding prairie and coulees. The adjacent Saskatchewan Landing Provincial Park is a staging area for migratory birds. Interpretive trails through aspen parkland and prairies, sandy beaches and active sand dunes are some of the attractions at Lake Diefenbaker.

Great Blue Heron

Last Mountain Lake

Grasslands, parkland and marshes converge at Last Mountain Lake, just north of Regina, to create a unique environment. Interpretive kiosks, self-guided nature trails and a bird observation tower await wildlife watchers. Because it is located on the central North American Flyway, up to 40,000 sandhill cranes, 400,000 snow geese and 250,000 ducks may pass through the area during peak spring or autumn migration times. Visitors, volunteers and bird banders are welcome at Last Mountain Bird Observatory, Saskatchewan's only bird observatory. At the north end of the lake is Last Mountain Lake National Wildlife Area, the oldest federal bird sanctuary on the continent.

Sandhill Crane

Road Duster Grasshopper

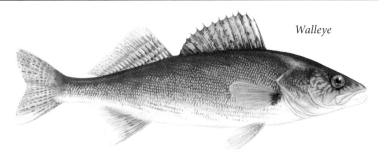

Walleye

Prince Albert National Park

Prince Albert National Park is found in lake country, where the aspen parkland meets the boreal forest. This park features cultural treasures, including the remote cabin of conversationalist Grey Owl. Natural wonders include a free-ranging herd of plains bison and Canada's only fully protected colony of nesting white pelicans. Pike, perch and walleye live in the many lakes, attracting grebes and common loons. Hundreds of kilometres of groomed snowmobile trails, cross-country ski trails, hiking trails and angling opportunities attract visitors year-round.

Royal Saskatchewan Museum

The provincial museum, located in Regina, offers year-round educational opportunities, interactive learning displays and a native plant garden in summer. The Life Sciences Gallery features an extensive collection of Saskatchewan plant and animals, and highlights Saskatchewan's landscapes throughout the seasons.

Canada Anemone

Wadena Wildlife Wetlands

Located in the Quill Lakes area, Wadena Wildlife Wetlands host the "Shorebirds and Friends Festival" the last weekend in May. The area supports breeding American white pelicans, avocets and several waterfowl species. Visitors can enjoy hiking trails, observation towers and interpretive signs. During spring and autumn migration, hundreds of thousands of snow geese, shorebirds and waterfowl pass through.

American White Pelican

37

SELECT MANITOBA WILDLIFE WATCHING SITES

We are truly blessed by Manitoba's geographical and biological diversity. Indeed, the province is quickly acquiring a reputation as one of North America's wildlife watching hotspots. Because it is near the geographic centre of the continent, Manitoba is home to northern and southern species as well as wildlife and plants from the east and the west. From the rugged Canadian Shield, lush grasslands and rolling parklands to Hudson Bay and the agricultural plains of the southern parts, Manitoba offers diverse and accessible wildlife viewing sites. The following areas have been selected to represent a broad range of communities and habitats, with an emphasis on diversity and accessibility.

PRAIRIE

1. Upper Assiniboine WMA
2. Poverty Plains, Mixed-grass Prairie Preserve and Broomhill WMA
3. Oak/Plum lakes
4. Lauder Sandhills
5. Alexander–Griswold Marsh
6. Minnedosa pothole region
7. Assiniboine River Trail (Brandon)
8. Brandon Hills
9. Souris River Bend WMA
10. Whitewater Lake
11. Turtle Mountain PP
12. Pembina Valley
13. Pelican Lake
14. Tiger Hills
15. Glenboro Marsh
16. Spruce Woods PP
17. Pinkerton Lakes
18. Portage Sandhills WMA
19. Crescent Lake (Portage la Prairie)
20. Lake Manitoba Narrows
21. Delta Marsh and St. Ambroise PP
22. Lake Francis
23. Narcisse Snake Dens WMA
24. Oak Hammock Marsh
25. Beaudry PP
26. Assiniboine Park and Fort Whyte (Winnipeg)

BOREAL PLAINS

27. Tall Grass Prairie Preserve
28. Rat River WMA and St. Malo WMA
29. Birds Hill PP
30. Netley–Libau Marsh

31. Hecla/Grindstone PP
32. Interlake area and Mantagao Lake WMA
33. Dog Lake
34. Crane River
35. Waterhen River
36. Riding Mountain NP
37. Duck Mountain PP
38. Porcupine PF
39. Clearwater Lake PP

MIXED WOOD SHIELD

40. Spur Woods WMA
41. Moose Lake PP and Birch Point PP
42. Mars Hill WMA
43. Grand Beach PP
44. Whiteshell PP and Pinawa area

BOREAL SHIELD

45. Nopiming PP
46. Grass River PP
47. Paint Lake/ Pisew Falls PP

TAIGA SHIELD

48. Sand Lakes PP

HUDSON PLAINS AND SOUTHERN ARCTIC

49. Churchill
50. Wapusk NP

PF = Provincial Forest
PP = Provincial Park
NP = National Park
WMA = Wildlife Management Area

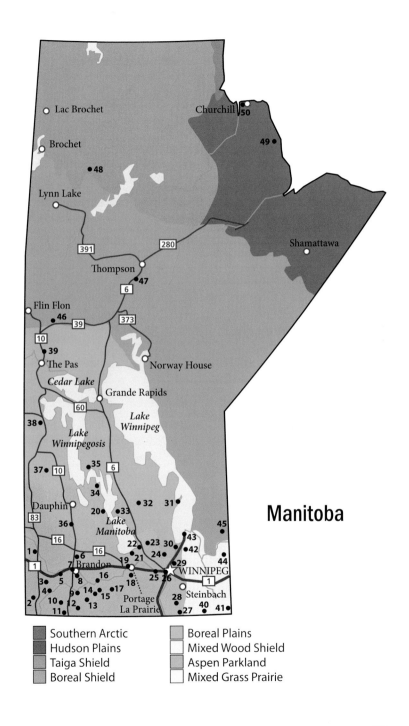

Manitoba

Southern Arctic
Hudson Plains
Taiga Shield
Boreal Shield

Boreal Plains
Mixed Wood Shield
Aspen Parkland
Mixed Grass Prairie

Yellow
Warbler

Assiniboine Park & Forest

Assiniboine Park is a unique, well-known forest within the city of Winnipeg. This large, productive, popular wildlife watching spot borders the Assiniboine River to the west of downtown. Its open, wooded lawns, lush aspen-oak forest, gardens and ponds are home to a herd of white-tailed deer and attract a wide variety of birds—5 vireo, 16 sparrow and 27 warbler species have been seen here. A well-maintained trail system provides year-round access to the park, and an observation area overlooks Eve Werier Memorial Pond.

Churchill

In recent years, the Churchill area has become a mecca for tourists, for its polar bears, beluga whales, bearded, ringed and harbour seals, wildflowers, northern lights displays and birdlife. Situated on the southern shore of Hudson Bay, where marine, tundra and coniferous forest habitats converge, the Churchill area offers innumerable wildlife-watching and plant-study opportunities. During the short summer months, more

Polar Bear

than 500 varieties of beautiful arctic wildflowers bloom briefly under the midnight sun. In June, when the ice breaks on Hudson Bay, birdwatchers can enjoy rafts of sea ducks, including species found nowhere else in Manitoba, such as the common eider (*Somateria mollissima*). Farther inland, scan the skies for soaring falcons, snowy owls or nesting shorebirds.

Clearwater Lake Provincial Park & Grass River Provincial Park

These two readily accessible northern parks, located between The Pas and Flin Flon, are a transition between the Manitoba Lowlands and Canadian Shield landscapes, and they abound with wildlife. Excursions by canoe will reveal common loons, a variety of waterfowl, pelicans, double-crested cormorants, bald eagles and belted kingfishers. The crystal clear lake is lined with sandy beaches and is home to trophy-sized trout, pike and whitefish. If you are travelling on land,

Double-crested Cormorant

hiking trails offer good opportunities to meet moose, bears, deer, spruce grouse, gray jays, pileated woodpeckers and nesting songbirds, including more than 20 colourful warblers and vireos. A self-guided trail leads to the impressive caves—400-million-year-old natural rock crevices where hardy plants survive in near darkness.

Common Cattail

HECLA/GRINDSTONE PROVINCIAL PARK

Hecla/Grindstone Provincial Park is composed of a series of peninsulas, islands and adjacent waters in Lake Winnipeg. The varied landscape includes coniferous and mixed forests, limestone cliffs, sandy beaches and wetlands. Boardwalks, viewing towers and viewing blinds at Grassy Narrows Marsh provide access for observing marshland species up close. As well as providing opportunities to learn about the geology and natural history of the area, these parks protect Aboriginal cultural sites and preserve an Icelandic fishing village.

Pileated Woodpecker

NARCISSE SNAKE DENS WILDLIFE MANAGEMENT AREA

The Narcisse Snakes Dens are one of Manitoba's natural wonders, truly a must-see for all nature lovers. Each spring, tens of thousands of red-sided garter-snakes emerge from their winter dens (hibernacula) to mate. Smaller, male snakes vie for the larger females, amassing in wriggly reptilian balls. After mating, the snakes disperse into the forest for the summer. They return in autumn, to hibernate underground in crevices in the limestone bedrock.

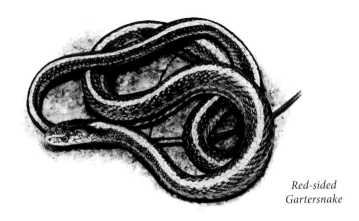

Red-sided Gartersnake

Oak Hammock Marsh

In terms of biodiversity, wetlands are second only to rainforests. Wetland plants provide the vegetative bedrock that supports myriad invertebrates, such as crayfish and dragonflies, which then provide fodder for higher animals. Pike, white sucker, carp, stickleback, shiners, several amphibian species, snapping turtles and painted turtles live in and around Oak Hammock Marsh, as do coyotes, badgers, muskrats, beavers and many birds.

This restored marsh is only a remnant of an extensive marshland that once existed. It is still one of the best migratory bird viewing areas in North America, however, and some 285 birds, including over 90 nesting species, have been recorded at Oak Hammock Marsh. Huge flocks of waterfowl, sandhill cranes, shorebirds and a variety

Beaver

of raptors pass through on migration, as do tens of thousands of snow geese and Canada geese. Common summer residents include the great blue heron, American bittern, and an array of shorebirds, waterfowl and grassland birds.

Oak Lake–Plum Lakes

Baltimore Oriole

The Oak Lake–Plum Lakes complex, located 60 km west of Brandon, is what remains of Lake Souris in the wake of glaciers that retreated here some 12,000 years ago. A wooded ridge at the east edge of Oak Lake is home to a small cottage development, but there is still a rich variety of wildlife, including deer, beavers, muskrats and many bird species such as ruby-throated hummingbirds, brown thrashers and Baltimore orioles.
Oak Lake is stocked with perch and northern pike. Plum Lake Marsh is a staging area for many species of waterfowl during spring and autumn migration.

Paint Lake Provincial Park & Pisew Falls Provincial Park

Pisew Falls and nearby Paint Lake, located 65 km south of Thompson in the Precambrian Shield, offer glimpses of black bear, moose, mink, otter and marten, spruce grouse, various woodpeckers, vireos, warblers and sparrows. Outdoor enthusiasts can explore the many islands, bays, sandy beaches or fish for walleye and northern pike.

American Marten

POVERTY PLAINS, BROOMHILL WILDLIFE MANAGEMENT AREA & MIXED-GRASS PRAIRIE PRESERVE

Manitoba's mixed-grass prairie is found in the extreme southwest of the province in the Poverty Plains area that stretches from Broomhill to Lyleton. While much of the area is privately owned, there is public access to the Mixed-grass Prairie Preserve in the heart of the Poverty Plains and to several local wildlife management areas, including Broomhill, Bernice and Pierson. Open pasturelands, haylands and mixed-grass prairie support impressive concentrations of grassland and woodland birds, including nesting sharp-tailed grouse and gray partridges, and many songbirds. Two-third of Manitoba's population of nesting endangered ferruginous hawks (*Buteo regalis*) and loggerhead shrikes (*Lanius ludovicianus*) are found in the area. Burrowing owls have been found here, and field shelterbelts in the Lyleton area support, among other species, orioles and brown thrashers.

Prairie Crocus

RIDING MOUNTAIN NATIONAL PARK

Riding Mountain, Manitoba's first national park, is situated about an hour north of Brandon and rises dramatically from the prairie landscape. This park includes boreal forest, a tract of eastern deciduous forest, rough fescue grasslands and numerous wetlands. The park houses a captive herd of bison, as well as black bears, wolves, elk, moose and numerous smaller mammals. Approximately 260 species of birds have been seen here.

Sharp-tailed Grouse

Moose

Turtle Mountain Provincial Park

Amidst the beautiful, rolling landscape of Turtle Mountain Provincial Park (which includes more than 200 lakes and 1000 smaller wetlands), visitors can engage in cross-country skiing, mountain biking, canoeing, hiking, camping and,

Western Painted Turtle

of course, wildlife viewing. Located southeast of Brandon along both sides of the Assiniboine River, this large park is blessed with a unique and intriguing mix of rolling sand dunes, native prairie, mixed forests, creeks, ponds and mature riparian woodlands. These diverse habitats, made accessible by the park's extensive system of trails, support quite an array of wildlife and plants, including some of the largest oak trees in Manitoba. Noteworthy animals include the moose, white-tailed deer, raccoon, loons and grebes. The shallow, nutrient-rich water bodies support western painted turtles and many fish species.

Rainbow Trout

Whiteshell Provincial Park & Nopiming Provincial Park

These popular parks are part of a rolling landscape of granite outcroppings topped by mixed boreal forest and interlaced by a network of streams, lakes, bogs and ponds. Located just over an hour's drive east of Winnipeg, Whiteshell Provincial Park is a 2729 km² tract of wilderness on the Canadian Shield. The 200 or so clear, cool lakes and many rivers abound with walleye, rainbow trout, lake trout and the occasional monster-sized northern pike. Black bear, deer, fox, otter and skunk are common here, as are snapping and painted turtles, gartersnakes, frogs, toads and myriad birds and insects.

Black Bear

ANIMALS

Animals are mammals, birds, reptiles, amphibians, fish and invertebrates, all of which belong to the Kingdom Animalia. They obtain energy by ingesting food that they hunt or gather. Mammals and birds are endothermic, meaning that body temperature is internally regulated and will stay nearly constant despite the surrounding environmental temperature unless that temperature is extreme and persistent. Reptiles, amphibians, fish and invertebrates are ectothermic, meaning that they do not have the ability to generate their own internal body temperature and tend to be the same temperature as their surroundings. Animals reproduce sexually, and they have a limited growth that is reached at sexual maturity. They also have diverse and complicated behaviours displayed in courtship, defence, parenting, playing, fighting, eating, hunting, in their social hierarchy, and in how they deal with environmental stresses such as weather, change of season or availability of food and water. We have included the region's most common, wide-ranging, charismatic or historically significant animals and have chosen a few representatives for diverse families such as rodents.

Big Brown Bat

MAMMALS

Mammals are the group to which human beings belong. The general characteristics of a mammal include being endothermic, bearing live young (with the exception of the platypus), nursing their young and having hair or fur on their bodies. In general, all mammals larger than rodents are sexually dimorphic, meaning that the male and the female are different in appearance by size or other diagnostics such as antlers. Males are usually larger than females. Different groups of mammals are either herbivores, carnivores, omnivores or insectivores. People often associate large mammals with wilderness, making these animals prominent symbols in Native legends and stirring emotional connections with people in modern times.

Marine Mammals
pp. 48–49

Bison
p. 50

Hoofed Mammals
pp. 50–52

Pronghorn
p. 53

Cats
pp. 53–54

Skunks & Weasels
pp. 55–58

Raccoon
p. 58

Bears
p. 59

Dogs
pp. 60–61

Porcupine
p. 62

Mice, Rats & Kin
pp. 62–64

Muskrat & Beaver
p. 65

Squirrels
pp. 66–70

Hares & Rabbits
pp. 70–71

Bats
pp. 72–74

Moles & Shrews
pp. 74–75

Beluga

Delphinapterus leucas

Length: up to 5.5 m; average 4 m
Weight: up to 1600 kg;
average 820 kg

Graceful belugas are social animals that often swim in small pods (social groups). A thick layer of blubber insulates them from frigid waters, and the lack of a dorsal fin helps them avoid being battered by sea ice. They are difficult to see because they spend most of their time underwater. Also known as "sea canaries," these vocal whales communicate, navigate and find prey using a series of twitters, chirps and whistles. • Occasionally bowhead whales and, in most years, killer whales are also seen along the Manitoba coast because climate warming is causing the waters in western Hudson Bay to become ice-free earlier. **Where found:** Hudson Bay.

Harbour Seal

Phoca vitulina

Length: 1.7 m
Weight: 100 kg

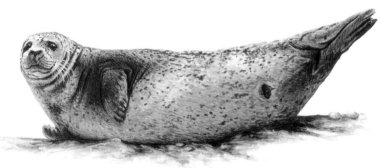

Groups of harbour seals are found throughout the Northern Hemisphere, including along both of Canada's coasts. They are fond of freshwater and often come into bays and estuaries or follow river systems well inland. The northern Manitoba population spends the winter inland, occasionally venturing up to 240 km upstream of Hudson Bay. • Adult harbour seals have small round heads, slightly upturned noses and unique white mottling. They are graceful swimmers but are clumsy on land. **Where found:** Hudson Bay and inland, along the freshwater river systems of northern MB.

Ringed Seal

Pusa hispida

Length: 1.2–1.7 m
Weight: 50–110 kg

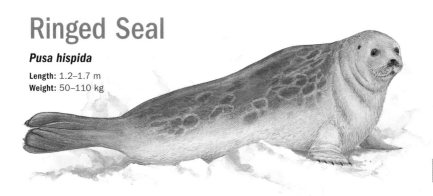

Ringed seals, the smallest and most common seals found in the Arctic, are closely associated with sea ice. In winter they are often found close to shore and, as a result, are important to the traditional Inuit culture and diet. • For protection against freezing temperatures and predators such as polar bears and arctic foxes, pregnant females hollow out a snow den under ice ridges. The fluffy, white pups are born in spring but turn a silvery grey once they are weaned, at about 8 weeks. At this time, females and pups abandon the den, and large groups bask on the sea ice and moult. Otherwise, ringed seals are largely solitary. **Where found:** northeastern MB, on or near sea ice in Hudson Bay.

Bearded Seal

Erignathus barbatus

Length: 2–3 m
Weight: 200–350 kg

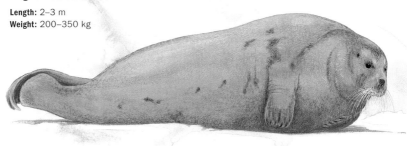

Bearded seals are named for the long, thick whiskers that they use to search the ocean bottom for food. These benthic feeders prefer shallow water, and solitary individuals may show up anywhere along the Manitoba coast during ice-free months. They prefer moving ice floes and are seldom seen on land. • During breeding season, males gather on communal display grounds and serenade females. Their long trilling calls can carry underwater for up to 25 km. • Unlike other seals, females give birth to twins and breed once every 2 years. **Where found:** shallow waters of Hudson Bay.

Bison

Bison bison

Length: 2.4–3.9 m
Shoulder height: 1.6–1.8 m
Weight: *Male:* 642–910 kg; *Female:* 493–567 kg

North America's largest native land mammal, the bison literally weighs a tonne! Before the arrival of the Europeans, great herds totalling millions of bison roamed parts of western North America. By the early 1900s, overhunting, disease, severe winters and interbreeding had devastated their numbers and extirpated these noble beasts from much of their range. Today, the vast majority of bison are raised in private herds, with Saskatchewan being the second largest producer of bison meat. Only a few wild, free-ranging or semi-wild herds remain, protected in parks over a patchy range.
• Two subspecies exist: the wood bison *(B. b. athabascae)* and the plains bison *(B. b. bison).* **Where found:** Select parks including Prince Albert NP and Buffalo Pound PP in SK and Riding Mountain NP in MB.

North American Elk

Cervus elaphus

Length: 1.8–2.7 m
Shoulder height: 1.7–2.1 m
Weight: 180–500 kg

The impressive bugle of the male North American elk once resounded throughout much of the continent, but the advance of civilization pushed these animals west. Today, elk are common in the Rocky Mountains and are scattered locally in the prairies.
• During the autumn mating season, rival males use their majestic antlers to win and protect a harem of females. An especially vigorous bull might command more than 50 females. After the rut, bull elk can put on as much as 1 kg every 2–3 days if conditions are good. The extra weight helps them survive the winter. **Where found:** grasslands or open woodlands; scattered locally through central and western SK (including Qu'Appelle Valley) and central and southwestern MB (including Riding Mt and Duck Mt parks). **Also known as:** wapiti.

White-tailed Deer

Odocoileus virginianus

Length: 1.4–2.1 m
Shoulder height: 70 cm–1.1 m
Weight: 30–115 kg

White-tailed deer populations have boomed in many areas. Easily our most abundant hoofed mammal, they are even found in urban and suburban areas, often near forested tracts, wooded ravines or river valleys. One herd lives right in the middle of Winnipeg, in Assiniboine Park. When startled, white-tails bound away flashing their conspicuous white tail. • Feeding does (females) leave their speckled, scentless fawns in dense vegetation to hide them from predators. • Bucks (males) regrow their racks, or antlers, each year and can develop massive racks with age. • The white-tailed is Saskatchewan's provincial animal emblem. **Where found:** most habitats except the densest forests; central and southern SK/MB.

Mule Deer

Odocoileus hemionus

Length: 1.3–1.9 m
Shoulder height: 90 cm–1.1 m
Weight: 31–215 kg

Gentle and often approachable, mule deer frequent open areas or parks, where they are wonderful to watch. They travel with a characteristic, bouncing gait, launching off and landing on all fours at the same time. • As their name suggests, mule deer have very large ears. Their white rump patch and black-tipped tail distinguishes them from white-tailed deer. **Where found:** open coniferous woodlands, grasslands, river valleys; central and southern SK and southwestern MB; threatened in MB. **Also known as:** black-tailed deer.

Moose

Alces alces

Length: 2.5–3 m
Shoulder height: 1.7–2.1 m
Weight: 230–540 kg

Moose are deer, and darn big ones—the world's largest. These impressive beasts have long legs that help them navigate bogs or deep snow. They can run as fast as 55 km/hr, swim continuously for several hours, dive to depths of 6 m and remain submerged for up to 1 minute. • Saplings with the tops snapped off and other damaged plants are signs that a moose stopped by for lunch. This animal is a voracious eater—an individual might consume 7250 kg of vegetation annually. **Where found:** coniferous forests, young poplar stands, willows; throughout.

Caribou

Rangifer tarandus

Length: 1.4–2.3 m
Shoulder height: 90 cm–1.7 m
Weight: 90–110 kg

Caribou are amazing animals that migrate hundreds of kilometres over harsh terrain. They draw the energy for their incredible journey from a diet of mainly lichens, grass and moss. Each year, these nomadic animals follow the available food supply, moving between protected winter habitat in the northern coniferous forests and summer calving grounds in the open tundra, where there are few predators. Their name originates from the Mi'kmaq word *halibu*, meaning "pawer" or "scratcher," because they feed by digging through the snow with their broad hooves to expose lichens. **Where found:** mature coniferous forests and tundra of central and northern SK/MB.

Pronghorn

Antilocapra americana

Length: 1.7–2.5 cm
Shoulder height: 85 cm–1 m
Weight: 32–63 kg

Capable of reaching speeds of up to 90 km/hr, the pronghorn is the fastest land mammal in North America and the second fastest in the world, after the cheetah. A large heart and lungs relative to its body size, an efficient metabolism and lack of a dewclaw are all adaptations for speed. Though swift, the pronghorn is a poor jumper, and the fencing of the prairies in the early 1900s lead to population declines. Today's fences are modified with enough space for pronghorn to slip underneath. • Pronghorn are sometime called antelope, but they in fact have no close living relatives. The male's pronged horns are unique; each year only the outer keratin sheath is shed, not the bony core. **Where found:** grasslands of southwestern SK.

Cougar

Puma concolor

Length: 1.5–2.7 m
Shoulder height: 65–80 cm
Weight: 30–90 kg

Cougars are skilled hunters with specialized teeth and claws for capturing prey; their sharp canines can kill a moose or deer in one lethal bite. • These nocturnal hunters can travel an average of 10 km per night. Historically, cougars were found throughout most of southern Canada, with a range overlapping that of deer, their favourite prey. With the coming of settlers, cougars were pushed out. Cougars are rare but possibly increasing in Saskatchewan and Manitoba. They have recently been spotted near Saskatoon, Moose Jaw, the Qu'Appelle Valley and Weyburn in Saskatchewan and near Riding Mountain Park and Duck Mountain Park in Manitoba. **Where found:** variety of habitats that provide cover; southern SK/MB.

Canada Lynx

Lynx canadensis

Length: 80 cm–1 m
Shoulder height: 45–60 cm
Weight: 7–18 kg

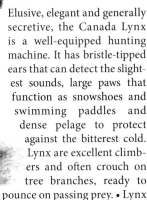

Elusive, elegant and generally secretive, the Canada Lynx is a well-equipped hunting machine. It has bristle-tipped ears that can detect the slightest sounds, large paws that function as snowshoes and swimming paddles and dense pelage to protect against the bitterest cold. Lynx are excellent climbers and often crouch on tree branches, ready to pounce on passing prey. • Lynx populations fluctuate every 7 to 10 years with snowshoe hare numbers. When hares are plentiful, lynx kittens are more likely to survive and reproduce; when there are fewer hares, more kittens starve and the lynx population declines. **Where found:** coniferous forests of northern SK/MB.

Bobcat

Lynx rufus

Length: 75 cm–1.25 m
Shoulder height: 45–55 cm
Weight: 7–13 kg

The bobcat has the widest distribution of any native cat in North America and ranges from southern Canada to central Mexico. The bobcat is not well adapted to deep snow and is replaced by the Canada lynx in the northern part of its range. All bobcats have dark streaks or spots, but their coat varies from yellowish to rusty brown or grey, depending on habitat and season. • This nocturnal hunter occupies a variety of habitats including deserts, wetlands and, surprisingly, developed areas. A feline speedster, it can hit 48 km for short bursts. The similar-looking lynx has longer ear tufts and a longer, black-tipped tail. **Where found:** southern SK/MB.

Striped Skunk

Mephitis mephitis

Length: 53–76 cm
Weight: 1.9–4.2 kg

Equipped with a noxious spray that can be
aimed up to 6 m, the striped skunk gives both humans and animals alike an over-
powering reason to avoid it. But come spring, when the mother skunk emerges
with her fluffy, 2-toned babies trotting behind her, you may find yourself enjoying
her company—from a distance. Skunk families typically den in hollow logs or
rock piles in summer then switch to old woodchuck or badger burrows for winter.
Where found: moist urban and rural habitats, including hardwood groves and
agricultural areas; throughout, except extreme north.

American Marten

Martes americana

Length: 56–66 cm
Weight: 500 g–1.2 kg

Much smaller than the similar fisher and mink,
the American marten's relatively diminutive
size allows it to use woodpecker cavities for
dens, which it often does. The marten prefers
coniferous forests but also ranges into mixed hardwood forests. Because it is
active during the day, the marten is more likely to be seen than other weasels. It
feeds mainly on small rodents but also consumes fish, snakes, small birds or eggs,
carrion and sometimes berries. • The marten was prized for its soft, luxurious fur.
Trapping combined with habitat loss has contributed to the species' decline.
Where found: mature coniferous forests; central and northern SK/MB.

Fisher

Martes pennanti

Length: 79 cm–1.1 m
Weight: 2–5.5 kg

Like all members of the weasel family, fishers are aggressive,
capable predators. But fishers are misnamed: although they can
swim well, they rarely eat fish, preferring snowshoe hares and
other small mammals. Fishers are one of the few
animals that regularly kill porcupines,
adeptly flipping them to gain access
to the soft, unprotected belly region.
• Fishers have specially adapted ankle bones that allow them
to rotate their feet and climb down trees headfirst. These reclusive animals prefer
intact wilderness and disappear once development begins. **Where found:** dense
coniferous and mixedwood forests; uncommon in central and northern SK/MB.

Least Weasel

Mustela nivalis

Length: 15–23 cm
Weight: 28–70 g

Woe to the hiding vole that has one of these miniscule barbarians charge into its burrow. The least weasel regularly invades holes in search of prey, and it eats up to its weight in food each day to fuel its incredibly fast metabolism. This small, mainly nocturnal carnivore is rarely seen, but you may glimpse one dashing for cover when you move a hay bale or piece of plywood. • Unlike the larger weasels, the least weasel has a much shorter tail with no black tip. **Where found:** open fields, forest edges, rock piles, abandoned buildings; throughout.

Short-tailed Weasel

Mustela erminea

Length: 25–33 cm
Weight: 45–105 g

If short-tailed weasels were the size of black bears, we'd all be dead. These voracious, mainly nocturnal predators tend to kill anything they can take down, especially mice and voles. A typical glimpse is of a small, eel-like mammal bounding along then vanishing before a positive ID can be made. • The short-tailed weasel's coat becomes white in winter, but the tail is black-tipped year-round. **Where found:** dense coniferous and mixed forests, shrub lands, meadows and riparian areas; throughout except extreme south. **Also known as:** ermine, stoat.

Long-tailed Weasel

Mustela frenata

Length: 30–46 cm
Weight: 85–400 g

Like other mustelids, long-tailed weasels exhibit serial-killer tendencies, killing more than they can consume. Excess prey is sometimes cached for later use. Capable hunters, these hyperactive beasts can bring down prey twice their size, though their normal fare consists of small vertebrates, insects and, occasionally, fruit. • Like other true weasels, the long-tailed turns white in winter, but the tip of the tail remains black. **Where found:** open, grassy meadows, brushland, woodlots, forest edges, fencerows; central and southern SK/MB.

Mink

Mustela vison

Length: 47–70 cm
Weight: 600 g–1.4 kg

Because mink were once coveted for
their silky fur, over trapping led
to localized declines of mink
populations. Today, most mink coats are made from ranch-raised animals. • The
mink moves with graceful, fluid motions, resembling a ribbon as it winds along
the shorelines. Rarely found far from water, the mink has webbed feet, making it
an excellent swimmer and diver that often hunts for underwater prey. Its thick,
dark brown to blackish, oily fur insulates the body from extremely cold waters.
• Mink travel along established hunting routes, sometimes resting in a muskrat
lodge after eating the original inhabitant. **Where found:** shorelines of lakes,
marshes, streams; throughout.

Black-footed Ferret

Mustela nigripes

Length: 45 cm
Weight: 1 kg

Our only native ferret is also one of the
most endangered mammals in North

America. Black-footed ferrets live in grasslands, where they coexist with prairie dogs,
their main prey. These ferrets were once believed to be globally extinct, but a small
population was found in Wyoming in 1981. Some black-footed ferrets have been captive bred and reintroduced to the United States. Black-footed ferrets have been
extirpated from Canada but historically reached the northern edge of their range in
southwestern Saskatchewan and southeastern Alberta. A reintroduction program
is proposed for autumn 2009. **Where found:** grasslands with prairie dogs; extirpated.

Wolverine

Gulo gulo

Length: 70 cm–1.1 m
Weight: 7–16 kg

From afar, a wolverine can look like a small
brown bear, until its long, bushy tail and
golden sides are revealed. This muscular animal
is capable of taking down a caribou or moose, but it usually scavenges carrion left
behind by larger predators. With its powerful jaws, the wolverine can crunch through
bone to access the nourishing marrow, leaving little trace of a carcass. It also eats
small animals, fish, bird eggs and berries. With a fondness for plastic and for mark-
ing landmarks with musk and urine, a wolverine can wreak havoc on unoccupied
exploration camps. • Chances of seeing this elusive animal are slim, even in the
most remote areas. **Where found:** remote boreal forest and northward.

Badger

Taxidea taxus

Length: 64–89 cm
Weight: 5–11 kg

This burly, burrowing beast is like a mammalian auger. A badger at full whirl sends a continuous plume of sediment skyward, quickly disappearing underground. Equipped with huge claws, strong forelimbs, powerful jaws and a pointed snout, the badger pursues subterranean dwellers such as ground squirrels, mice and snakes. • Badger holes are essential in providing den sites, shelters and hibernacula for many creatures, from coyotes to black-widow spiders. **Where found:** low-elevation fields, meadows, grasslands, fencelines, ditches; central and southern SK/MB.

Northern River Otter

Lontra canadensis

Length: 90 cm–1.4 m
Weight: 5–11 kg

Playful otters are extremely entertaining, whether you are watching them at the zoo or are lucky enough to see them in the wild. Their long, streamlined bodies, fully webbed feet and muscular tails make them swift, effortless swimmers with incredible fishing ability. • River otters are highly social animals, usually travelling in small groups. Good clues to their presence are "slides" on the shores of water bodies or troughs in the snow created by tobogganing otters. **Where found:** near lakes, ponds, streams; throughout.

Raccoon

Procyon lotor

Length: 65 cm–1 m
Weight: 5–14 kg

These black-masked bandits are common in many habitats, including suburbia, and are often found near water. When on the move, raccoons present a hunch-backed appearance and run with a comical, mincing gait. Although they are not true hibernators, they become sluggish during colder weather and may hole up for extended periods. These agile climbers are often seen high in trees or peeking from arboreal cavities. • Raccoons are known for wetting their food before eating, a behaviour that allows them to feel for and discard inedible matter. **Where found:** wooded areas near water; southern SK/MB.

Black Bear

Ursus americanus

Length: 1.4–1.8 m
Shoulder height: 90 cm–1.1 m
Weight: 40–270 kg

Don't be fooled by the clumsy, lumbering gait of a black bear. Deceptively speedy, this bear can hit 50 km/hr for short bursts. It is also an excellent swimmer and can climb trees. • The black bear is omnivorous, eating an incredibly varied diet and exploiting whatever food source is at hand. During much of the year, up to three-quarters of its diet may be vegetable matter. • One of the few North American mammals that truly hibernates, the black bear packs on the fat, then retires to a sheltered den for winter. Vegetable matter in its pre-hibernation diet forms an anal plug, preventing expulsion during the bear's long slumber. **Where found:** forests and open, marshy woodlands; throughout central and northern SK/MB.

Polar Bear

Ursus maritimus

Length: 2–3.4 m
Shoulder height: 1.2–1.6 m
Weight: *Male:* 300–800 kg;
Female: 150–300 kg

Equipped with layers of fat, hollow, white guard hairs and black skin, polar bears are well adapted to icy waters and subzero temperatures. • Cubs born in midwinter spend their first 3 months in a snow den, suckling on their mother's warm milk. They emerge in early May and spend their first 28 months with their mother, learning how to survive and hunt seals on the arctic ice packs. • Recent climate change models predict drastic changes in the distribution and thickness of the sea ice that polar bears and seals depend on for hunting, denning and resting. **Where found:** Hudson Bay and up to 100 km inland; world-famous viewing at Churchill, MB.

Coyote

Canis latrans

Length: 1–1.3 m
Shoulder height: 58–66 cm
Weight: 10–22 kg

Occasionally forming loose packs and joining in spirited yipping choruses, coyotes are clever and versatile hunter-scavengers. They often range into suburbia and even live in densely populated cities. This dog-like mammal has benefited from large-scale habitat changes, booming in numbers and greatly expanding its range. Also, widespread eradication of predators such as grey wolves has helped coyotes flourish. • The coyote has a smaller, thinner muzzle than the wolf, and its tail drags behind its legs when it runs. **Where found:** open woodlands, agricultural lands, near urban areas; throughout.

Grey Wolf

Canis lupus

Length: 1.5–2 m
Shoulder height: 66–97 cm
Weight: 38–54 kg

Wolves have been perse-cuted since the first Euro-peans entered North America and have been eradicated from vast areas of their former range. The animals' large size, fierce predatory behaviour, pack-forming habits and the role they play in fables such as Little Red Riding Hood have instilled fear in many people. Today, however, the approximately 6000 wolves in Saskatchewan and Manitoba are valued symbols of the wilderness and are crucial to a healthy, balanced food chain. • Wolf packs co-operate within a strong social structure that is dominated by an alpha pair (dominant male and female). **Where found:** boreal forests and taiga of central and northern SK/MB. **Also known as:** timber wolf.

Arctic Fox

Alopex lagopus

Length: 75–91 cm
Shoulder height: 25–30 cm
Weight: 1.8–4.1 kg

White in winter and bluish grey in summer, the arctic fox is the only member of the dog family that changes fur colour with the seasons. Uniquely adapted to the Arctic, this small fox has a dense, insulating coat, furry feet and acute hearing for tracking small animals under the snow. • The arctic fox feeds on polar bear or grey wolf kills, rodents, bird eggs and occasionally seal pups. During the plentiful summer months, this resourceful fox stores food for winter by digging a hole into the permafrost layer. **Where found:** taiga, tundra; northern SK/MB.

Swift Fox

Vulpes velox

Length: 80 cm
Shoulder height: 30 cm
Weight: 2.25–2.5 kg

North America's smallest wild dog, the swift fox is about the size of a house cat. This little fox disappeared from Canada in the 1930s as a result of drought, habitat loss, trapping and from eating poison meant for rodents and coyotes. In the 1970s, an Alberta couple began a captive-breeding program and, with the co-operation of prairie ranchers, the swift fox was reintroduced to its former grassland habitat. About 300 swift foxes live in the Canadian prairies today. • This opportunistic hunter feeds mainly on small rodents and carrion and is in turn taken by coyotes, eagles and hawks. • Unlike other species of fox, the swift fox uses its den year-round for protection and birthing. **Where found:** dry grasslands; southern SK/MB; endangered.

Red Fox

Vulpes vulpes

Length: 90 cm–1.1 m
Shoulder height: 38 cm
Weight: 3.6–6.8 kg

Most red foxes are a rusty reddish brown, but rare variations include blackish forms and even a silvery type. These small animals look like dogs but often act like cats: they stalk mice and other small prey and make energetic pounces to capture victims. • Dens are typically in old woodchuck burrows or similar holes. Tracks are often the best sign foxes are present: their small, oval prints form a nearly straight line. **Where found:** open habitats with brushy shelter, riparian areas, edge habitats; throughout.

Porcupine

Erethizon dorsatum

Length: 66–100 cm
Weight: 3.5–18 kg

Prickly porcupines are best left alone. Contrary to popular myth, they cannot throw their 30,000 or so quills, but with a lightning-fast flick of the tail, they'll readily impale some of their spikes into persistent attackers. • Porcupines clamber about trees, stripping off the bark and feeding on the sugary cambium layer. Although they are sure-footed, they aren't infallible; in one study, about one-third of museum specimen skeletons examined had old fractures, presumably from arboreal mishaps. • Porcupines crave salt and will gnaw on rubber tires, wooden axe handles, toilet seats and even hiking boots! **Where found:** coniferous and mixed deciduous-coniferous forests up to the subalpine; throughout except extreme north.

Meadow Jumping Mouse

Zapus hudsonius

Length: 19–22 cm
Weight: 15–25 g

Like tiny kangaroos, jumping mice can leap almost 1 m when startled. They have large hind feet, powerful rear legs and a long tail to help them balance as they jump. Mostly found in damp meadows, they can be identified by their distinctive mode of locomotion. • Meadow jumping mice hibernate for 6 to 7 months in underground burrows, one of the longest periods of any North American mammal. Their metabolism slows and they survive on stored fat deposits. • The western jumping mouse (*Z. princeps*) is common in central and southern SK/MB. **Where found:** prefers fields; also forest edges, marshes, streambanks; throughout except southern SK.

Brown Rat

Rattus norvegicus

Length: 30–46 cm
Weight: 200–480 g

The mammalian counterpart to house sparrows, these introduced rats thrive around human settlements. Native to Europe and Asia—but not Norway—the brown rat came to North America stowed away on early ships. • Brown rats can carry parasites and diseases transferable to wildlife, humans and pets, but captive-bred rats have given psychologists many insights into human learning and behaviour. • Wild brown rats have brown to reddish brown, often grizzled pelage with grey tones and grey undersides. **Where found:** urban areas, farmyards, garbage dumps; throughout. **Also known as:** Norway rat, common rat, sewer rat, water rat.

House Mouse

Mus musculus

Length: 14–19 cm
Weight: 14–25 g

Chances are, if you have a mouse in your
house, it is a house mouse. This species
has been fraternizing with humans for several thousand years. Like the brown rat,
it stowed away on ships from Europe, quickly spreading across North America with
settlers. • House mice are gregarious and social, even grooming one another. They
are destructive in dwellings, however, shredding insulation for nests, leaving drop-
pings and raiding pantries. • These tiny beasts have brownish to blackish grey backs
and grey undersides. **Where found:** usually associated with human settlements,
including houses, garages, farms, garbage dumps, granaries; throughout.

Deer Mouse

Peromyscus maniculatus

Length: 12–18 cm
Weight: 18–35 g

This abundant mouse often occupies cavities
in trees, stumps and logs, old buildings and bluebird nest boxes, where it builds
a dense nest of plant matter. These little critters are strong swimmers, and they
often brave the water to colonize islands. They primarily eat nuts, berries, seeds,
vegetation and insects, but will also raid your pantry. • Similar to the white-
footed mouse (*P. leucopus*) of southern Saskatchewan, the deer mouse is pale to
dark reddish brown above, white below and has protruding ears and a bicoloured
tail. **Where found:** various habitats including woodlands, riparian areas, shrubby
areas, some farmlands; common throughout except extreme north.

Meadow Vole

Microtus pennsylvanicus

Length: 14–20 cm
Weight: 18–64 g

Meadow voles rank high among the world's most
prolific breeders. If unchecked by predators, they
would practically rule the earth. • Little furry sausages
with legs, meadow voles are important food for raptors, especially in winter. Their
populations have cyclical highs and lows, and in boom years impressive numbers
of hawks and owls will congregate in good vole fields. Primarily active at night,
this common vole can be seen during the day as well, especially when populations
are high. • The Gapper's red-backed vole (*Clethrionomys gapperi*) and the heather
vole (*Phenacomys intermedius*) are also common throughout much of our region.
Where found: open woodlands, meadows, fields, fencelines, marshes; throughout.

Northern Bog Lemming

Synaptomys borealis

Length: 11–14 cm
Weight: 27–35 g

Lemmings look rather like voles but have larger, rounded heads. They live primarily in extensive systems of subsurface tunnels and feed mainly on grasses and sedges. Neatly clipped piles of grass along paths, and their curious green scat, indicate northern bog lemmings are nearby. Lemmings remain active during winter, tunnelling through the subnivean layer—along the ground, under the snow. • Populations can vary from year to year, and in boom years especially, they are a major prey item for predators. The southern bog lemming (*S. cooperi)* occurs in southeastern Manitoba. **Where found:** burrows among sedges and grasses, moist spruce forests, sphagnum bogs; throughout central and northern regions.

Ord's Kangaroo Rat

Dipodomys ordii

Length: 26 cm, including tail
Weight: 68–71 g

With the aid of its extra-long tail, the Ord's kangaroo rat can leap 1.8 m to avoid predators. These nocturnal mammals have acute hearing, tuned to detect an owl's wingbeat. • Ord's kangaroo rats live among sand dunes, surviving on seeds that they collect in their fur-lined cheek pouches. In Canada, they occupy only about 50 km ^{2} of open, arid, sand dunes on the southern Saskatchewan-Alberta border, a habitat that is rapidly shrinking as a result of climate change and human encroachment. **Where found:** sparsely vegetated grassland and sandy areas of the Grand Sand Hills area of southwestern SK; endangered.

Olive-backed Pocket Mouse

Perognathus fasciatus

Length: 10–15 cm
Weight: 8–14 g

The tiny olive-backed pocket mouse will explode into motion when threatened, sometimes leaping 60 cm vertically. It has large hind legs and small forelegs and moves in an unusual hop, using all 4 limbs. • This specialized rodent inhabits open, sandy, thinly vegetated grasslands. Considered the slowest of all rodents, it spends much of the day grooming itself in an underground burrow but becomes active at dusk. **Where found:** open, active sand dunes; southern SK and southwestern MB.

Muskrat

Ondatra zibethicus

Length: 14–61 cm
Weight: 800 g–1.6 kg

More comfortable in water than on land, the muskrat has a laterally compressed tail that allows it to swim like a fish. Its occurrence in wetlands is easily detected by the presence of cone-shaped lodges made from cattails and other vegetation. • Muskrats play an important role in marsh management by thinning out dense stands of cattails. They also vex marsh managers by digging burrows in dikes. In general, muskrats are quite valuable in wetland ecosystems, creating diversified habitats that benefit many other species. **Where found:** lakes, marshes, ponds, rivers, reservoirs, dugouts, canals; throughout.

Beaver

Castor canadensis

Length: 91 cm–1.2 m
Weight: 16–30 kg

No mammal influences its environment to the degree that this jumbo rodent—North America's largest—does. Its complex dams are engineering marvels that create ponds and wetlands for a diversity of flora and fauna. The presence of conical, gnawed stubs of tree trunks is a sure sign a beaver is present. With a loud warning slap of its tail on water, the beaver often disappears before it is detected. • Beavers were nearly exterminated in many areas at one time, trapped prolifically for their valuable pelts. They have made an amazing comeback and are once again common. **Where found:** lakes, ponds, marshes, slow-flowing rivers and streams; throughout.

Least Chipmunk

Tamias minimus

Length: 17–23 cm
Weight: 35–71 g

Scampering along forest paths between hollowed-out logs, this cute, curious rodent has the widest distribution of the 22 North American species of chipmunks. Its habitat ranges from sagebrush deserts to alpine tundra. This incurable seed gatherer plays an important role in forest ecology. In addition to hoarding food in its burrow, the least chipmunk often "loses" acorns and other fruit, helping to distribute plants. • Although chipmunks more or less hibernate from autumn until spring, they wake every few weeks to feed, even coming above ground in mild weather. • The reddish brown eastern chipmunk (*T. striatus*) occurs in southern Manitoba. **Where found:** campgrounds, coniferous forests, pastures, rocky outcroppings; throughout except extreme southwestern SK.

Woodchuck

Marmota monax

Length: 46–66 cm
Weight: 1.8–5.4 kg

Burly woodchucks have powerful claws for digging burrows up to 15 m long. Most people are used to seeing woodchucks scuttling along on the ground, so it is a surprise to find them high up a tree, but they are squirrels, after all. More typically, they graze along forest edges and clearings, using their sharp incisors to rapidly cut plants, bark and berries. • Woodchucks are true hibernators and spend much of the year tucked away underground. Groundhog Day (February 2) celebrates their emergence. **Where found:** meadows, pastures, open woodlands; central and southern MB. **Also known as:** groundhog.

Red Squirrel

Tamiasciurus hudsonicus

Length: 28–34 cm
Weight: 140–250 g

This pugnacious and vocal squirrel often drives larger squirrels and birds from bird feeders, and sometimes takes bird eggs and nestlings. It can eat highly poisonous *Amanita* mushrooms and will bite into sugar maple bark to feed on sap. Large middens of discarded pine cone scales are evidence of its buried food bounty. • The red squirrel may chatter, stomp its feet, flick its tail and scold you with a piercing cry. • During the short spring courtship, squirrels engage in incredibly acrobatic chases. **Where found:** coniferous and mixed forests; throughout.

Eastern Grey Squirrel

Sciurus carolinensis

Length: 43–50 cm
Weight: 400–710 g

Originally a species of large, mature forests, grey squirrels now thrive in suburbia. Their large, roundish nests are made primarily of leaves and are often quite conspicuous in trees, but their winter den sites and birthing locales are in tree cavities. • Active all year, grey squirrels can locate their nut caches several months later, even those that are buried under snow. About 10 to 20% of hidden nuts are forgotten; many will grow into trees. • In some areas, melanistic or black forms predominate. Occasional albinos turn up, and these white squirrels become local celebrities. **Where found:** mature deciduous or mixed forests with nut-bearing trees; uncommon and local in SK, increasingly common in southeastern MB. **Also known as:** black squirrel.

Fox Squirrel

Sciurus niger

Length: 53 cm
Weight: 790 g

Robust fox squirrels have richer orange and yellowish over-tones to their pelage than grey squirrels and are up to twice as bulky. They wave their bushy, fox-like tails about when excited. They often have favourite spots to which they bring food, and such sites are littered with nutshells. • Fox squirrels spend more time on the ground than grey squirrels and are sometimes seen far from trees. An individual fox squirrel may have a home range of 20 ha; a grey squirrel's range usually does not exceed 2 ha. Relative newcomers to Saskatchewan, fox squirrels are expanding their range from Manitoba and North Dakota. **Where found:** mature deciduous or mixed forests with nut-bearing trees; southern SK/MB.

Northern Flying Squirrel

Glaucomys sabrinus

Length: 24–36 cm
Weight: 75–180 g

Long flaps of skin (called the "patagium") stretched between the fore and hind limbs and a broad, flattened tail allow this nocturnal flying squirrel to glide swiftly from tree to tree. After landing, the squirrel inevitably hustles around to the opposite side of the trunk in case a predator, such as an owl, has followed. • The flying squirrel plays an important role in forest ecology because it digs up and eats truffles, the fruiting bodies of ectomycorrhizal fungus that grows underground. Through its stool, the squirrel spreads the beneficial fungus, helping both the fungus and the forest plants. **Where found:** primarily old-growth conifer-ous and mixed forests; throughout except extreme north and south.

Thirteen-lined Ground Squirrel

Spermophilus tridecemlineatus

Length: 18–30 cm
Weight: 110–270 g

Highly social, these squirrels live in
colonies and construct complex
underground labyrinths to retreat to
when threatened. From October to March, they retire into their burrows, singly or
communally, spending winter curled up into tight balls. During hibernation, their
respiration decreases from 100 to 200 breaths per minute to 1 breath every 5 minutes.
Where found: prairie, abandoned fields, mowed lawns, agricultural areas; locally
common in central and southern SK/MB. **Also known as:** striped gopher.

Richardson's Ground Squirrel

Sciurus richardsonii

Length: 25–36 cm
Weight: 370–480 g

Familiar prairie inhabitants, Richardson's ground squirrels (more
commonly called "gophers") issue shrill whistles and habitually flick
their tails. They are often seen sitting upright at their burrow
entrance or scampering through roadside ditches. • Their burrows
are hidden in the dense grass of open prairies and fields. Some
authorities believe these squirrels spend up to 90% of their lives
underground. • The Franklin's ground squirrel (*S. franklinii*)
has a noticeably bushy tail and occurs in central and southern SK/MB's tall or mid-grass prairie. **Where found:** prairie,
meadows, pastures; southern half of SK, southwestern MB.

Black-tailed Prairie Dog

Cynomys ludovicianus

Length: 35–50 cm
Weight: 500 g–1.5 kg

Highly social black-tailed prairie dogs live together in colonies
and spend much of their time underground. These burrowing
mammals provide important habitat for, and increase diversity
of, many grassland species ranging from burrowing owls to
arthropods. Prairie dogs are also important prey items for
numerous species, including eagles, ferruginous hawks, prairie rattlesnakes and
foxes. Across their range, from southern Saskatchewan to Chihuahua, Mexico,
they are threatened by disease and habitat loss and are generally considered
unwelcome pests, often hunted or poisoned by landowners. **Where found:** in and
adjacent to Grasslands NP, SK; special concern.

Northern Pocket Gopher

Thomomys talpoides

Length: 25–28 cm
Weight: 185 g

Supremely adapted for underground living, this mammalian Rototiller (often incorrectly called a "mole") has naked feet equipped with long front claws for digging, furred lips that extend over long incisor teeth to prevent dirt from entering its mouth while eating and digging, and fur-lined cheek pouches for the temporary storage of roots, tubers and green plants. • A pocket gopher's incisor teeth grow as much as 1 mm a day. If unchecked by constant gnawing, the lower incisors could grow 36 cm in a year! • The plains pocket gopher *(Geomys bursarius)* occurs in the Roseau River area, near Emerson, MB, but nowhere else in Canada. **Where found:** various habitats, including agricultural fields, grasslands, shrub lands, suburban lots; southern half of SK southwestern MB.

Snowshoe Hare

Lepus americanus

Length: 38–53 cm
Weight: 1–1.5 kg

Snowshoe hares are completely adapted for life in snowy conditions. Large, snowshoe-like feet enable them to traverse powdery snow without sinking. Primarily nocturnal, they blend perfectly with their surroundings regardless of the season. They are greyish, reddish or blackish brown in summer, and white in winter. • If detected, the hare explodes into a running zigzag pattern in its flight for cover, reaching speeds of up to 50 km/hr on hard-packed snow trails. • In Manitoba, this species is replaced by the larger Arctic hare *(Lepus arcticus)* along the Hudson Bay coast. **Where found:** brushy or forested areas; throughout. **Also known as:** varying hare.

White-tailed Jackrabbit

Lepus townsendii

Length: 48–70 cm
Weight: 2.7–4 kg

The speedy white-tailed jackrabbit is capable of 70-km/h sprints to outrun potential predators. Before taking flight, it sits motionless with its ears laid flat over its back. Recent clearing of forests has created new habitat for this species. • Unlike rabbits, which give birth to altricial young and hide from danger, hares give birth to precocial young capable of running nearly from birth. • This jackrabbit's buffy to brownish grey pelage turns white in winter. Its undersides, hind feet and tail remain white, and the long ears are black-tipped all year. **Where found:** grasslands, shrub lands, sagebrush; central and southern SK/MB.

Nuttall's Cottontail

Sylvilagus nuttallii

Length: 34–40 cm
Weight: 700 g–1 kg

The Nuttall's cottontail is our smallest member of the rabbit family. • Adapted to the arid prairie grasslands, the cottontail avoids daytime predators by hiding under rocks, machinery or in dugout depressions under thorny buffaloberry or similar shrubs. It emerges at dusk to graze on grasses and forbs, sagebrush or juniper berries, but the cottontail never strays far from cover. Parks such as Grasslands National Park in southern Saskatchewan offer intimate viewing opportunities.
Where found: variety of habitats near shrubby cover; southern SK.
Also known as: mountain cottontail.

Eastern Cottontail

Sylvilagus floridanus

Length: 40–45 cm
Weight: 800 g–1.3 kg

Cottontails can have 7 litters annually, each of which can contain up to 9 young, and they reproduce at a very young age. One pair and all of their offspring could produce up to 350,000 rabbits over a span of 5 years. But predators enjoy eating them as much as humans do, and few survive their first year. • Eastern cottontails' amusing courtship displays involve males and females facing off and making fantastic vertical leaps, often hop-scotching over one another. **Where found:** variety of habitats near shrubby cover; southern MB.

Northern Bat

Myotis septentrionalis

Length: 8.3–10 cm
Forearm length: 3.3–4 cm
Weight: 3.5–8.9 g

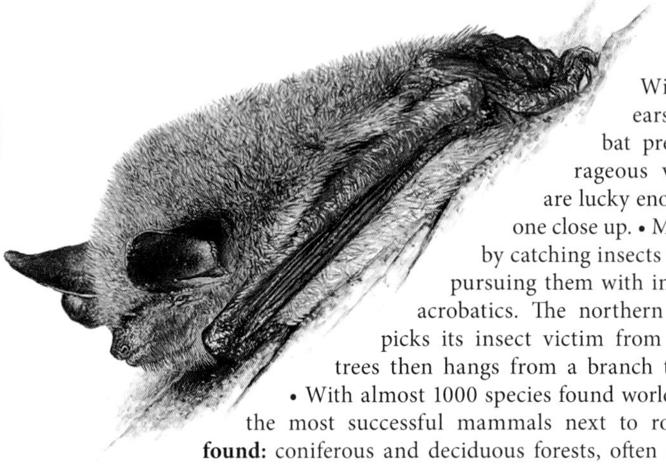

With Spock-like ears, the northern bat presents an outrageous visage—if you are lucky enough to admire one close up. • Most bats forage by catching insects while in flight, pursuing them with incredible aerial acrobatics. The northern bat, however, picks its insect victim from the foliage of trees then hangs from a branch to consume it. • With almost 1000 species found worldwide, bats are the most successful mammals next to rodents. **Where found:** coniferous and deciduous forests, often close to water; roosts in tree cavities, under peeling bark, in rock crevices; hibernates in caves, abandoned mines; locally common in central and southern SK/MB.

Little Brown Bat

Myotis lucifugus

Length: 7–10 cm
Forearm length: 3.5–4 cm
Weight: 5.3–9 g

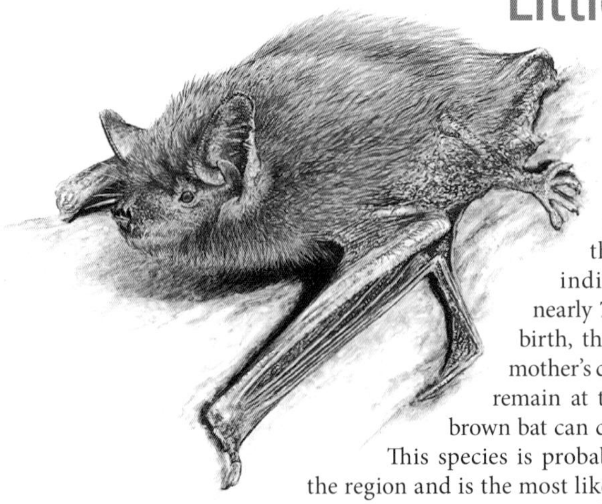

Each spring, these bats form maternal roosting colonies that can number thousands of individuals—one colony had nearly 7000 bats. Virtually helpless at birth, the single offspring clings to its mother's chest until it is strong enough to remain at the roost site. • A single little brown bat can consume 900 insects per hour. This species is probably the most common bat in the region and is the most likely to be seen at dusk. **Where found:** roosts in buildings, barns, caves, crevices, hollow trees, under tree bark; hibernates in buildings, caves, old mines; throughout.

Red Bat

Lasiurus borealis

Length: 8–13 cm
Forearm length: 3.75–4.5 cm
Weight: 7–14 g

This distinctive species roosts in tree foliage 1 to 3 m above the ground. Sometimes what looks like a reddish brown hanging leaf cluster suddenly turns into a red bat! • Red bats have long, slender wings and can reach 65 km/hr. These fast fliers are highly migratory, and animals in the northern parts of the range migrate south for winter. • Red bats feed on insects attracted to the illumination of streetlights. Look for their yellowish orange to red fur; the male's fur is brighter red. **Where found:** roosts on unobstructed branches that allow it to drop into flight; southern SK/MB in warmer months.

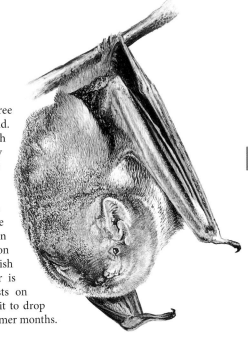

Hoary Bat

Lasiurus cinereus

Length: 11–15 cm
Forearm length: 4.5–5.7 cm
Weight: 19–35 g

Hoary bats are the most widely distributed—and arguably the most beautiful—bats in North America. Their large size and frosty silver fur make them quite distinctive. Identify them at night by their size and slow wingbeats over open terrain. • These bats roost in trees, not caves or buildings, and wrap their wings around themselves for protection against the elements. They often roost in orchards, but they are insectivores and do no damage to fruit crops. **Where found:** roosts on branches of coniferous and deciduous trees, occasionally in tree cavities; migrates south for winter; throughout.

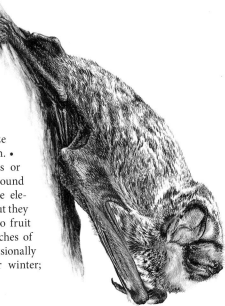

Silver-haired Bat

Lasionycteris noctivagans

Length: 9–11 cm
Forearm length: 3.8–4.5 cm
Weight: 7–18 g

Silver-haired bats are most likely to be found roosting under a loose piece of bark. Sometimes they occur in small, loosely associated groups. • These bats mate in autumn, but actual fertilization doesn't occur until spring. This odd strategy ensures that plenty of food will be available when their young are born. • To conserve energy on cold days, they can lower their body temperature and metabolism—a state known as "torpor." • This bat's black flight membrane can span 30 cm. **Where found:** roosts in cavities and crevices of old-growth trees; migrates south for winter; southern SK/MB.

Big Brown Bat

Eptesicus fuscus

Length: 9–14 cm
Forearm length: 4.5–5.5 cm
Weight: 12–28 g

This bat's ultrasonic echolocation (20,000 to 110,000 Hz) can detect flying beetles and moths up to 5 m away. It flies above water or around streetlights searching for prey, which it scoops up with its wing and tail membranes. • Few animals rest as much as bats, and they can live for many decades as a result of the low stresses on their physiological systems. After spending 2 or 3 hours on the wing each evening, they perch and their body functions slow down for the rest of the day. **Where found:** in and around artificial structures, occasionally roosting in hollow trees, rock crevices; hibernates in caves, mines, old buildings; central and southern SK/MB.

Star-nosed Mole

Condylura cristata

Length: 15–21 cm
Weight: 30–75 g

Looking like it collided headfirst with a tiny sea anemone, the star-nosed mole looks bizarre, to say the least. The 22 anemone-like appendages ringing its snout are actually extremely sensitive "feelers." Each fleshy appendage can be collapsed or extended individually and moves continuously in all directions, serving as an effective detector of prey. **Where found:** prefers wet areas such as marshes, low fields, humid woodlands; southeastern MB.

Masked Shrew

Sorex cinereus

Length: 7–11 cm
Weight: 2–7 g

This mammal is one of our most abundant—but good luck seeing one. Mostly nocturnal and prone to scurrying about in dense cover, this voracious shrew consumes its body weight or more in food daily. To balance high late-winter mortality rates and year-round predation, a female may have 2 to 3 litters per year, giving birth to as many as 8 blind, toothless and naked young at a time. • The arctic shrew (*S. arcticus*) is common in central and northern regions. **Where found:** forests, occasionally tall-grass prairies; throughout except southwestern SK. **Also known as:** cinereus shrew.

Northern Water Shrew

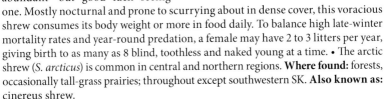

Sorex palustris

Length: 13–17 cm
Weight: 9–19 g

The water shrew has large feet fitted with stiff, bristly hairs that allow it to run across the water's surface for a surprising distance. Thick, insulating body fur traps air bubbles between the hairs and allows it to hunt aquatic invertebrates in cold ponds and streams. Robust for a shrew, it catches small fish and tadpoles that other shrews cannot. • The coat is dark, velvety brown to black with whitish grey undersides and a distinctive, bicoloured tail. **Where found:** fast-flowing streams, lakes, ponds, marshes with vegetated shorelines; throughout except extreme south. **Also known as:** water shrew.

Pygmy Shrew

Sorex hoyi

Length: 11–13 cm
Weight: 2–7 g

The pygmy shrew is our smallest mammal and weighs no more than a penny. • This pennyweight shrew stands up on its hind legs, curiously like a bear. • Because of its size and secretive habits, the pygmy shrew is seldom observed, at least not well enough to be identified. • Shrews have an incredibly high metabolic rate, with heart rates often reaching 1200 beats per minute. Most of the heat energy they produce is quickly lost, so pygmy shrews routinely eat 3 times their body weight in a day, taking down and consuming any prey that can be overpowered. **Where found:** various habitats, from forests to open fields, sphagnum bogs; throughout except extreme southwestern SK.

BIRDS

Birds are the most diverse class of vertebrates. All birds are feathered but not all fly. Traits common to all birds are that they are 2-legged, warm-blooded and lay hard-shelled eggs. Some migrate south in the colder winter months and return north in spring. For this reason, the bird diversity of Saskatchewan and Manitoba varies with the seasons. Spring brings scores of migrant waterfowl and colourful songbirds that breed in the region and other birds such as shorebirds that continue on to arctic breeding grounds. Even more migratory birds pass through in autumn, their numbers bolstered by young of the year. Many are in duller plumage at this time, and they are largely silent. Scores of migrating birds fly as far south as Central and South America. These neotropical migrants are of concern to biologists and conservationists because habitat degradation and loss, collisions with human-made towers, pesticide use and other factors threaten the birds' survival. Education and increasing appreciation for wildlife may encourage solutions to these problems.

Waterfowl
pp. 78–82

Grouse & Allies
p. 83

Diving Birds
pp. 84–85

Herons & Vultures
p. 86

Birds of Prey
pp. 87–88

Rails & Coots
p. 89

Cranes
p. 89

Shorebirds
pp. 90–91

Gulls & Allies
pp. 92–93

Pigeons & Doves
p. 93

Owls
p. 94–95

Nighthawks
p. 96

Hummingbirds & Kingfishers
p. 96

Woodpeckers
p. 97

Flycatchers
p. 98

Shrikes & Vireos
p. 99

Jays & Crows
pp. 99–101

Larks & Swallows
p. 102

Chickadees & Nuthatches
p. 103

Wrens
p. 103

Bluebirds & Thrushes
p. 104

Mimics, Starlings & Waxwings
pp. 104–05

Wood-warblers
pp. 106–07

Sparrows & Grosbeaks
pp. 107–08

Blackbirds & Allies
pp. 109–10

Finch-like Birds
pp. 110–11

Snow Goose

Chen caerulescens

Length: 71–84 cm
Wingspan: 1.4–1.5 m

Noisy flocks of snow geese fly in wavy, disorganized lines, and individuals give a loud, nasal *houk-houk* in flight, higher pitched and more constant than Canada geese. Snow geese breed in the Arctic, some travelling as far as northeastern Siberia and crossing the Bering Strait twice a year. These common geese have all-white bodies and black wing tips. An equally common colour morph, the "blue goose" has a dark body and white head, and was considered a distinct species until 1983. **Where found:** croplands, fields, marshes; migrant, Apr–May and Sept–Nov.

Canada Goose

Branta canadensis

Length: 92 cm–1.2 m
Wingspan: up to 1.8 m

Few avian spectacles rival that of immense flocks of migratory Canada geese. The collective honking of airborne groups can be heard for 2 km or more. • This species varies throughout its range, and in 2004 was split into 2 species. The large subspecies are Canada geese, and the smaller, mallard-sized birds are cackling geese. The latter is scarcer in our region. Canada geese are probably the most instantly recognizable species of waterfowl in North America. **Where found:** lakeshores, riverbanks, ponds, farmlands, city parks; throughout, Apr–Nov.

Tundra Swan

Cygnus columbianus

Length: 1.2–1.5 m
Wingspan: 1.8–2.1 m

As waters begin to thaw in early April, noisy tundra swans arrive in our southern prairies to feed in flooded agricultural fields and pastures. Swans have all-white wings, unlike snow geese, which have black wing tips. • Other than the rare trumpeter swan, this species is the largest native bird in our region—adults can weigh 7 kg. It would take about 2075 ruby-throated hummingbirds to equal the weight of a tundra swan, illustrating the dramatic diversity of the bird world. **Where found:** shallow areas of lakes and wetlands, flooded agricultural fields, pastures; migrant, Apr and Oct–Nov.

Wood Duck

Aix sponsa

Length: 38–50 cm
Wingspan: 76 cm

In the early 20th century, many ornithologists predicted the extinction of this beautiful duck. Sound hunting regulations and improvement in habitat, in part as a result of the recovery of the beaver, aided this species' remarkable comeback. • The wood duck is the best known of our cavity-nesting ducks, and thousands of nest boxes placed across its breeding range have greatly increased populations. • Shortly after hatching, ducklings jump out of their nest cavity, falling up to 15 m to bounce harmlessly like ping-pong balls on landing. **Where found:** wetlands, rivers, lakeshores with wooded edges; central and southern SK/MB, Apr–Oct.

Mallard

Anas platyrhynchos

Length: 51–71 cm
Wingspan: 76 cm

The male mallard, with its shiny green head, chestnut brown breast and stereotypical quack, is one of the best-known and most commonly seen ducks. • Mallards are extremely adaptable and become semi-tame fixtures on suburban ponds. They remain year-round wherever open water is available. • After breeding, male ducks lose their elaborate plumage, helping them stay camouflaged during their flightless period. In early autumn, they moult back into breeding colours. **Where found:** widespread in various water bodies; common throughout Mar–Nov, uncommon and local in winter.

Blue-winged Teal

Anas discors

Length: 36–41 cm
Wingspan: 58 cm

Blue-winged teals are quite speedy on the wing and are able to execute sharp twists and turns, often just above the water's surface. These dabbling ducks lurk in dense marsh vegetation and can be overlooked. Watch for a white crescent patch next to the male's bill, visible in all plumages. As is typical with waterfowl, females are much duller, providing camouflage as they incubate eggs on a ground nest. **Where found:** shallow lake edges, wetlands, flooded fields; throughout, Apr–Oct.

Northern Pintail

Anas acuta

Length: *Male:* 64–76 cm;
Female: 51–56 cm
Wingspan: 86 cm

Elegant and graceful both on water and in the air, the Northern Pintail is a beautiful bird. The male's 2 long, pointed tail feathers are easily seen in flight and point skyward when the bird tips up to dabble. • Northern pintails are the most widely distributed duck in the world. Despite impressive numbers in our region, drought, wetland drainage and changing agricultural practices are the most serious threats contributing to a slow population decline. **Where found:** shallow wetlands, flooded fields, lake edges; widespread, Apr–Oct.

Northern Shoveler

Anas clypeata

Length: 46–50 cm
Wingspan: 76 cm

The northern
shoveler has a green,
mallard-like head but is distinguished
by a much larger bill. • This duck dabbles on the surface for food and often stirs up shallow water with its feet, then submerges its head to feed. A shoveler pumps water into and out of its bill with its tongue, using the long comb-like structures (called lamellae) that line the sides of its bill to filter out food. **Where found:** wetlands, sloughs, lakes with muddy bottoms and emergent vegetation; throughout except extreme north and eastern MB; common in south, becoming uncommon northward, Apr–Oct.

Canvasback

Aythya valisineria

Length: 48–56 cm
Wingspan: 74 cm

Canvasbacks
can readily be
recognized by their "ski-slope nose"—the long tapered forehead flows smoothly into the long bill—and the bright white plumage on the males' back and sides. Like other male *Aythya* ducks—a sizeable genus of diving ducks of deep marshes, lakes and estuaries—male canvasbacks are "dark at both ends and pale in the middle." • Their scientific epithet refers to eel-grass *(Vallisneria americana)*, an aquatic plant. Canvasbacks congregate where beds of this submergent succulent occur. **Where found:** wetlands bordered by emergent vegetation; uncommon in central parts, fairly common in south, Apr–Oct.

Lesser Scaup

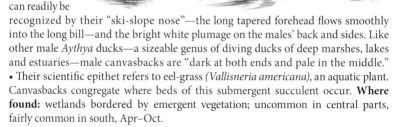

Aythya affinis

Length: 38–45 cm
Wingspan: 63 cm

Like an Oreo cookie,
scaups are white in the
middle and dark at both ends. Two similar looking species occur in our region, the lesser and greater scaup (*A. marila*), but it takes a lot of experience to reliably separate them in the field. • Lesser Scaups are the most abundant diving ducks in North America. They make up nearly 90% of the total scaup population, but for unknown reasons scaup populations—both lesser and greater—are decreasing by more than 150,000 birds a year. **Where found:** lakes, open marshes, along slow-moving rivers; throughout, Apr–Oct.

Common Goldeneye

Bucephala clangula

Length: 41–51 cm
Wingspan: 66 cm

Common golden-eyes are sometimes called "whistlers" because the drake's wings create a loud, distinctive hum in flight. • In mid-April, testosterone-flooded males begin their crazy courtship dances. Emitting low buzzes, drakes thrust their heads forward, lunge across the water and kick their brilliant orange feet forward like aquatic break-dancers. **Where found:** lakes, large ponds, rivers near mature forest; common in boreal forest, uncommon migrant on prairie, Apr–Nov.

Common Merganser

Mergus merganser

Length: 56–69 cm
Wingspan: 86 cm

Drake mergansers ride low in the water. Noticeably larger than most other species of ducks, these jumbos can tip the scales at 1.6 kg, making them one of our heaviest ducks. Mergansers' bills are sharply serrated, like carving knives, and are designed to seize fishy prey. • Outside of the breeding season, mergansers are highly social, forming large flocks. **Where found:** large forest-lined rivers, deep lakes, reservoirs; common in boreal forest, uncommon migrant on prairie, Apr–Nov.

Ruddy Duck

Oxyura jamaicensis

Length: 38–41 cm

Wingspan: 56–62 cm

This unusual little duck often holds its stiff tail upright. The drake is resplendent in breeding plumage, with a bright azure bill, a large white cheek patch and a rusty body. He inflates sacs in his neck during his courtship display, tilts his head backward and emits a series of notes. • Although the ruddy is one of our smallest ducks, the female lays enormous eggs—larger than a mallard's, even though a mallard is twice the size of a ruddy duck. **Where found:** prairie wetlands with emergent vegetation, Apr–Sept.

Gray Partridge

Perdix perdix

Length: 28–36 cm
Wingspan: 48 cm

Like other seed-eating birds, partridges regularly swallow small bits of gravel to help crush the hard seeds they feed on. The gravel accumulates in the birds' gizzard, a muscular pouch of the digestive system. • During cold weather, gray partridges huddle together in a circle with each bird facing outward, ready to burst into flight at the first sign of danger. These Eurasian game birds are relatively hardy, but many perish during harsh winters. They feed on grains and seeds, sometimes visiting rural bird feeders. **Where found:** weedy fields, agricultural lands, often near hedgerows; fairly common year-round on the prairie.

Ruffed Grouse

Bonasa umbellus

Length: 38–48 cm
Wingspan: 56 cm

Each spring, the male ruffed grouse proclaims his territory by strutting along a fallen log with his tail fanned wide and his neck feathers ruffed, beating the air with accelerating wing strokes. Drumming is primarily restricted to spring, but the ruffed grouse may also drum for a few weeks in autumn. • Ruffed grouse are well adapted to their northern environment. In autumn and early winter, scales on the sides of their toes grow out, creating temporary snowshoes. **Where found:** deciduous and mixed forests, riparian woodlands; undergoes cyclical fluctuations; year-round resident, absent from southwestern SK and northern SK/MB.

Sharp-tailed Grouse

Tympanuchus phasianellus

Length: 38–51 cm
Wingspan: 56–64 cm

In spring, male sharp-tailed grouse convene upon grassy knolls and shrubby forest clearings to perform courtship dances. With their long, thin tails pointed skyward, drooping wings and purplish pink air sacs inflated, the males furiously stamp their feet, vigorously cooing and cackling to attract females. Air release through their mouths from the inflated neck sacs produces a cooing sound that can be heard for several hundred metres. The dominant males dance in the centre of the "lek." • The sharp-tailed grouse is the provincial bird emblem of Saskatchewan. **Where found:** prairie, sagebush flats, agricultural areas; locally common year-round in southern SK/MB, uncommon elsewhere.

Common Loon

Gavia immer

Length: 71–89 cm
Wingspan: 1.2–1.5 m

The wild, yodelling cries of loons are a symbol of northern wilderness and evoke images of remote lakes. These graceful swimmers have nearly solid bones that decrease their buoyancy (most birds have hollow bones), and their feet are placed well back on their bodies to aid in underwater propulsion. Small bass, perch and sunfish are all fair game for these excellent underwater hunters that will chase fish to depths of up to 55 m. **Where found:** large lakes, rivers; fairly common in boreal forest, uncommon on prairie, Apr–Nov.

Red-necked Grebe

Podiceps grisegena

Length: 43–56 cm
Wingspan: 56 cm

Grebes carry their newly hatched, striped young on their backs. The young can stay aboard even when the parents dive underwater. • Grebes have individually webbed, or "lobed," feet. The 3 forward-facing toes have special flanges that are not connected to the other toes. **Where found:** lakes, ponds; breeds in emergent vegetation zone; fairly commonly in aspen parklands and northward, uncommon migrant in grasslands, May–Oct.

American White Pelican

Pelecanus erythrorhynchos

Length: 1.3–1.7 m
Wingspan: 3 m

Majestic American white pelicans breed in colonies in the Canadian prairies and the western United States, and they winter from the southern states to Guatemala, travelling between breeding and wintering areas in flocks of dozens of individuals. • The American white pelican feeds co-operatively, swimming in flocks and herding fish into shallow water. As a pelican lifts its bill from the water, the fish are held within the flexible pouch while the water drains, then the fish are swallowed whole. A pelican's pouch can hold up to 12 litres of water! **Where found:** rivers, freshwater lakes; central and southern SK/MB, Apr–Sept.

Double-crested Cormorant

Phalacrocorax auritus

Length: 66–81 cm
Wingspan: 1.3 m

Double-crested cormorants out-swim fish, which they capture in underwater dives. Most water birds have waterproof feathers, but the structure of the cormorant's feathers allow water in. "Wettable" feathers make this bird less buoyant and a better diver. It has sealed nostrils for diving, and therefore must occasionally open its bill to breathe while in flight. Cormorants feed mainly on shallow water, non-commercial fish such as suckers. **Where found:** large lakes; fairly common in southern two-thirds of SK/MB, Apr–Sept.

85

American Bittern

Botaurus lentiginosus

Length: 58–70 cm
Wingspan: 1.1 m

The cryptic American bittern inhabits marshes throughout our region. Its deep, resonate calls can be heard on spring nights, but this well-camouflaged bird tends to remain hidden. A threatened bittern freezes with its bill pointed skyward—its vertically streaked, brown plumage blends perfectly with the surrounding marsh. In most cases, intruders simply pass by without ever noticing the bird. • American bitterns are sensitive to human disturbance. Populations are declining across North America as a result of wetland habitat loss or degradation. **Where found:** marshes, wetlands, lake edges with tall, emergent vegetation; fairly common throughout, becoming rare northward, Apr–Sept.

Great Blue Heron

Ardea herodias

Length: 1.3–1.4 m
Wingspan: 1.8 m

The stealthy heron waits motionlessly for a fish or frog to approach, spears the prey with its bill, then swallows it whole. The heron usually hunts near water, but it also stalks fields and meadows in search of rodents. • Great blue herons settle in communal treetop nests called rookeries. Nesting herons are sensitive to human disturbance, so observe this bird's behaviour from a distance. **Where found:** along edges of rivers, lakes, marshes, fields, wet meadows; southern two-thirds of SK/MB, Apr–Oct.

Turkey Vulture

Cathartes aura

Length: 66–81 cm
Wingspan: 1.7–1.8 m

Turkey vultures rarely flap their wings, and they rock slightly from side to side as they soar. They hold their wings in a dihedral, or V-shaped position. Endowed with incredible vision and olfactory senses, turkey vultures can detect carrion, their only food source, at great distances. • Vultures often form communal roosts in trees, atop buildings, in barn lofts or on power line towers and will use the same roosting sites for decades. Do not approach a nest; turkey vultures vomit a decidedly unpleasant goop on invaders. **Where found:** habitat generalist; fairly common, local in southern half of SK/MB, Apr–Sept.

Bald Eagle

Haliaeetus leucocephalus

Length: 79 cm–1.1 m
Wingspan: 1.7–2.4 m

The majestic bald eagle is usually found near water. It preys on fish but is also an inveterate scavenger. • Bald eagles do not mature until their 4th or 5th year, when they develop the white head and tail plumage. They mate for life and reuse nests year after year, adding to them each season. Their aeries can grow to mammoth proportions, the largest of any North American bird. • Bald eagles were severely affected by DDT, a toxin that has long been banned in Canada. Eagle populations have increased dramatically ever since. **Where found:** large lakes, rivers; fairly common Apr–Nov, uncommon winter resident in south.

Northern Harrier

Circus cyaneus

Length: 41–61 cm
Wingspan: 1.1–1.2 m

In flight, this graceful raptor is unmistakable. It has a distinctive white rump patch and flies low over the ground with its wings raised in a slight dihedral. This bird's sudden appearance startles small prey such as voles, which are quickly pounced on. A perched northern harrier looks astonishingly like an owl: it has prominent facial discs to better detect and focus sounds. • Britain's Royal Air Force was so impressed by the northern harrier's maneuverability that it named the Harrier aircraft after this bird. **Where found:** open country, including fields, wet meadows, marshes; common on prairie and uncommon elsewhere, Apr–Oct.

Swainson's Hawk

Buteo swainsoni

Length: 48–51 cm
Wingspan: 1.3 m

The common buteo of the prairies, the Swainson's Hawk dominates the skies where ground squirrels are abundant. • Twice a year, the Swainson's hawk undertakes a long migration, from the tip of South America to as far north as Alaska. Travelling up to 20,000 km in a single year, the Swainson's hawk is second only to the arctic-breeding peregrine falcon (*Falco peregrinus*) for long-distance travel among birds of prey. • Pointed wing tips, slightly upturned wings and dark flight feathers differentiate the Swainson's hawk from all other raptors in flight. **Where found:** open fields, grasslands with scattered trees; common on prairie, Apr–Sept.

Red-tailed Hawk

Buteo jamaicensis

Length: *Male:* 46–58 cm; *Female:* 51–64 cm
Wingspan: 1.2–1.5 m

Common and widespread, Red-tailed hawks are often seen along country roads, perched on fences or trees, especially in the aspen parkland ecoregion. Their white breasts render them conspicuous. • The Red-tailed Hawk's impressive piercing call is often paired with the image of an eagle in TV commercials and movies. **Where found:** open country with some trees, roadsides, woodlots; common in south/central SK and southern MB, increasingly uncommon northward, Mar–Oct.

American Kestrel

Falco sparverius

Length: 23–30 cm
Wingspan: 50–62 cm

The colourful American kestrel frequently perches on roadside wires or hovers over fields like an avian helicopter. This little falcon feeds on small rodents and in warmer months switches to a diet heavy in grasshoppers. • Most evidence suggests that kestrel populations are declining significantly in many areas, partially because of a lack of nesting holes. You could help these cavity-nesting falcons by erecting appropriate nest boxes in suitable habitat. **Where found:** open fields, grassy roadsides, agricultural landscapes; common in boreal plains, uncommon and local elsewhere, Apr–Oct.

Merlin

Falco columbarius

Length: 25–35 cm
Wingspan: 60–68 cm

Using speed, surprise and sharp talons, the merlin often snatches songbirds in midair. This aerodynamic falcon is often seen flying low and fast over treed urban areas. Its noisy, cackling *kek-kek-kek-kek* call is heard in spring. • Most merlins migrate south each autumn, but some remain in the prairies for winter, enticed by mild urban climates and an abundance of songbirds at backyard feeders. **Where found:** treed areas next to open hunting grounds, suburban areas, lakeshores; uncommon to fairly common from Apr–Nov, rare to uncommon in south (mainly in cities) in winter.

Sora

Porzana carolina

Length: 20–25 cm
Wingspan: 30–36 cm

Two loud plaintive whistles, followed by a loud, descending whinny announces the presence of the sora. Although you have probably never seen a sora, this reclusive bird can be surprisingly abundant. • Rails have large, chicken-like feet for walking on aquatic vegetation, and they swim quite well over short distances. They can laterally compress their bodies to slip effortlessly through thick cattail stands. **Where found:** marshes, sloughs with abundant emergent vegetation; fairly common in north, common elsewhere, May–Sept.

American Coot

Fulica americana

Length: 33–40 cm
Wingspan: 58–70 cm

Sometimes called "mudhens," coots are the extroverts of the rail world. While the rest of the clan remains hidden in wetland vegetation, coots swim in open waters like ducks. Their individually webbed toes make them efficient swimmers and good divers, but they aren't above snatching a meal from another skilled diver. • In marshes where they breed, coots give loud, maniacal, laughing calls. **Where found:** shallow, open wetlands with emergent vegetation; common to abundant on prairie, becoming rare northward, Apr–Oct.

Sandhill Crane

Grus canadensis

Length: 1.1–1.2 m
Wingspan: 1.8–2.1 m

Sandhill cranes have deep, rattling calls that resonate from their coiled tracheas to carry great distances. Migrating flocks sail on thermal updrafts, circling and gliding at such great heights that they can scarcely be seen. In spring, cranes occasionally touch down on open fields to perform spectacular courtship dances, calling, bowing and leaping with partially raised wings. Large numbers can be seen during migration at Kindersley Outlook, Last Mountain, Quill Lakes (SK) and Whitewater Lake, Delta Marsh and Oak Hammock Marsh (MB). **Where found:** agricultural fields and shorelines during migration, Apr and Oct; mainly breeds in isolated northern bogs, Apr-Sept.

Killdeer

Charadrius vociferus

Length: 23–28 cm
Wingspan: 61 cm

When an intruder wanders too close to its nest, the killdeer puts on its "broken wing" display. It greets the interloper with piteous *kill-dee kill-dee* cries while dragging a wing and stumbling about as if injured. Most predators take the bait and follow, and once the predator has been lured far away from the nest, the killdeer flies off with a loud call. • This species has no doubt increased tremendously in modern times, as human activities have increased suitable habitat. **Where found:** open fields, lakeshores, gravel streambeds, parking lots, large lawns; throughout, Apr–Nov.

American Avocet

Recurvirostra americana

Length: 42–48 cm
Wingspan: 68–96 cm

Seeing an American avocet, with its peachy red head and neck, needle-like bill and bold black and white plumage, makes for a gold-letter day for many birders. The avocet inhabits saline lakes, flooded agricultural fields and mudflats. Its thin, upturned bill is the perfect shape for skimming food off the surface of the water or probing muddy shorelines for invertebrates. • Before autumn migration, large flocks of avocets stage at our larger, shallow lakes. At this time, their peachy hoods have been replaced by subtler winter greys. **Where found:** lakeshores, alkaline wetlands, exposed mudflats, prairie; throughout, May–Sept.

Spotted Sandpiper

Actitis macularia

Length: 18–20 cm
Wingspan: 38 cm

In a rare case of sexual role-reversal, the female spotted sandpiper is the aggressor. She diligently defends her territory and may mate with several males, an unusual breeding strategy known as "polyandry." • Each summer, the female can lay up to 4 clutches and is capable of producing 20 eggs. She lays the eggs but does little else—the males tend the clutches. • Spotted sandpipers bob their tails constantly while on shore and fly with rapid, shallow, stiff-winged strokes, like a wire under tension that has been "twanged." **Where found:** shorelines, gravel beaches, swamps, sewage lagoons; common throughout except in dry grasslands, May–Sept.

Lesser Yellowlegs

Tringa flavipes

Length: 25–28 cm
Wingspan: 71 cm

The lesser yellowlegs and greater yellowlegs *(T. melanoleuca)* are very similar medium to
large sandpipers. The lesser has a much finer, shorter
bill (about as long as its head width) and longer, thinner
legs. It normally delivers a pair of whistles, whereas the
greater utters a louder, more strident series of 3 or more whistles. The overall body
mass of a lesser is only half that of a greater, something very apparent when the species are together. • Yellowlegs are sometimes called "tell-tales": they alert all the
shorebirds on a mudflat to the presence of intruders, such as birders. **Where found:**
shallow wetlands, shorelines, flooded fields; common migrant on prairie, common
breeder in boreal forest and northward, Apr–Oct.

Wilson's Snipe

Gallinago delicata

Length: 27–29 cm
Wingspan: 46 cm

The winnowing of the Wilson's snipe is synony-
mous with spring evenings at a wetland. Snipes engage in
spectacular aerial courtship displays, swooping and diving
at great heights with their tails spread (the winnowing
sound is made by air rushing past the outer tail feathers).
• Well-camouflaged snipes are often concealed by vegetation. When flushed from
cover, the snipe utters a harsh *skape* note and then flies in a low, rapid zigzag pattern to confuse would-be predators. **Where found:** marshes, meadows, wetlands;
common except in dry grasslands, Apr–Sept. **Formerly:** common snipe.

Wilson's Phalarope

Phalaropus tricolor

Length: 21–24 cm
Wingspan: 36–40 cm

Phalaropes are the wind-up toys of
the bird world: they spin and whirl
about in tight circles, stirring up the water.
Then, with needle-like bills, they pick out the
aquatic insects and small crustaceans that funnel toward the surface. • With all
phalaropes, sexual roles are reversed; the larger, more colourful female may mate
with several males. The female lays the eggs, but the male incubates them and tends
the young. **Where found:** marshes, wet meadows, sewage lagoons, lakeshores
during migration; common on prairie, uncommon in central areas, May–Sept.

Franklin's Gull

Leucophaeus pipixcan

Length: 33–38 cm
Wingspan: 90 cm

Small and buoyant on the wing, the Franklin's gull is much different than its larger, cruder cousins. This common prairie gull nests on inland lakes and is only found along the coastlines in winter. It often follows tractors across agricultural fields, snatching up insects from the tractor's path; its cousins follow fishing boats in much the same way. **Where found:** agricultural fields, marshy lakes, landfills, river and lake shorelines; common in central areas, abundant in south, Apr–Sept.

Ring-billed Gull

Larus delawarensis

Length: 46–51 cm
Wingspan: 1.2 m

Few people can claim to have never seen this common, widespread gull. Highly tolerant of humans, the ring-billed gull eats almost anything and swarms parks, beaches, golf courses and fast-food restaurant parking lots looking for food handouts. It is a 3-year gull, first acquiring adult plumage in its third calendar year of life, after going through a series of subadult moults. **Where found:** small, barren islands during breeding, lakes, rivers, landfills, parking lots, fields, parks in migration; common to abundant in central and southern areas, uncommon in north, late Apr–Oct.

Common Tern

Sterna hirundo

Length: 33–40 cm
Wingspan: 76 cm

Common terns capture shiners and other small fish in spectacular aerial dives, plunging into the water from heights of 30 m or more. Groups sometimes follow schools of large fish that are feeding, snatching smaller fish that are flushed to the surface. • A courting male offers small fish to the female; if she accepts the gift, they pair up and nest. • In some places, breeding tern colonies have been detrimentally affected by large gulls that prey on their eggs and chicks. **Where found:** large lakes, slow-moving rivers, wetlands; rare in north, fairly common elsewhere, May–Aug.

Black Tern

Chlidonias niger

Length: 23–25 cm
Wingspan: 61 cm

Graceful black terns dip, swoop and dive above
cattail marshes and over adjacent fields, catching
insects in midair or picking them from the water's surface. • Wetland habitat loss and
degradation have caused black tern populations to decline. These birds are sensitive
nesters and will not return to a nesting area if the water level or plant density changes.
Wetland conservation efforts may eventually help them recover to their former pros-
perity. **Where found:** shallow marshes, wet meadows, sewage ponds with emergent
vegetation; rare in north, common and local elsewhere, May–Aug.

Rock Pigeon

Columba livia

Length: 31–33 cm
Wingspan: 71 cm

Formerly called rock doves, these Old World pigeons
are one of the world's most recognized birds. They
have been domesticated for about 6500 years;
because of their ability to return to far-flung locales, they
are often bred as "homing pigeons." • All pigeons and doves feed
their young a nutritious liquid, called "pigeon milk" (it's not real milk), that is produced in their crop • **Where found:** urban areas, railways, agricultural areas; abundant in south, uncommon northward, year-round.

Mourning Dove

Zenaida macroura

Length: 28–33 cm
Wingspan: 46 cm

The mourning dove is the leading game bird in North
America, with hunters taking up to 70 million doves
annually, but it remains one of the most abundant and
widespread native birds on the continent. An average
clutch usually has only 2 eggs, but doves raise multiple broods and breed nearly year-round in warmer
climates. • When the mourning dove bursts into
flight, its wings often create a whistling sound.
Where found: open woodlands, agricultural and suburban areas; abundant on
prairie, uncommon northward, Apr–Oct but may overwinter in south.

Great Horned Owl

Bubo virginianus

Length: 46–64 cm
Wingspan: 91 cm–1.5 m

Our most common large owl, the great horned owl occurs in all manner of habitats. This powerful predator can take mammals the size of small house cats and is one of the few predators of skunks. • Great horned owls begin their courtship as early as January, and by February or March, the females are incubating eggs. Most great horned owls nest on crow or hawk stick nests and may be spotted by their "ears" projecting above the nest. **Where found:** open agricultural landscapes, marshes with scattered woodlots, suburban areas; uncommon to fairly common year-round.

Snowy Owl

Bubo scandiacus

Length: 51–69 cm
Wingspan: 1.4–1.7 m

Feathered to its toes, the ghostly white snowy owl is well adapted to frigid winter temperatures. Its transparent feathers trap heat like a greenhouse, especially when ruffled out. • Male snowy owls stockpile lemmings at nest sites for foggy or rainy days when hunting is poor. Nests have been found in the Arctic with up to 56 lemmings piled nearby. When lemming and vole populations crash in the Arctic, more snowy owls venture south to search for food. **Where found:** open country, including forest clearings, agricultural areas, lakeshores; uncommon to fairly common except in boreal forest, Nov–Apr.

Short-eared Owl

Asio flammeus

Length: 38 cm
Wingspan: 96 cm

The short-eared owl flies low over wet meadows, often by day, beating its long wings with slow, butterfly-like wingbeats. • Short-ears perform spectacular aerial courtship dances while clapping their wing tips together below their bodies. These birds typically inhabit open country where these courtship displays—called sky dances—are more effective than the usual "hoot" for communicating. • This owl's life revolves around the population levels of voles, leading to nomadic movements in response to prey availability. **Where found:** open country, including grasslands, wet meadows, cleared forests; highly erratic; uncommon to fairly common year-round in southern SK; Mar–Nov elsewhere.

Burrowing Owl

Athene cunicularia

Length: 23–28 cm
Wingspan: 50–60 cm

Burrowing owls are loyal prairie inhabitants that nest underground in abandoned animal burrows. During the day, they may be seen atop fence posts or on the dirt mound beside their nest entrance. The extermination of tunnelling animals such as ground squirrels has greatly reduced owl nest sites. Other challenges include the loss of grassland habitat, the poisoning of prey species and the effects of agricultural chemicals. Species strongholds are the Regina Plains, the Cabri and Weyburn areas and Grasslands National Park. **Where found:** open, short-grass hayfields, pastures, prairie, occasionally lawns and golf courses; uncommon and local in southern SK and extreme southwestern MB, Apr–Sept; endangered.

Common Nighthawk

Chordeiles minor

Length: 22–25 cm
Wingspan: 61 cm

Displaying nighthawks put on dramatic aerial courtship displays. The male flutters high over nesting sites, uttering nasal *peent* notes, and then dives with his wings extended. At the bottom of the dive, wind rushing through the primary feathers produces a hollow, booming sound. • The nighthawk also feeds in midair. Feather shafts surrounding its large, gaping mouth funnel insects into its bill. • Resting nighthawks sit lengthwise on tree branches and can be nearly invisible. **Where found:** open and semi-open country, nests on rooftops in suburban, urban areas; uncommon in central parts, fairly common in south, May–Sept.

Ruby-throated Hummingbird

Archilochus colubris

Length: 9–9.5 cm
Wingspan: 11.5 cm

Aerial extremists, these hummingbirds can beat their wings several dozen times a second and, like tiny helicopters, fly in any direction. At full tilt, these nickel-weight speedsters have a heart rate of over 1000 beats per minute. Courting males fly a pendulum-like arc, creating a loud hum with their wings. • Hummingbirds are attracted to feeders and flower gardens. Their tiny lichen-shingled nests house 2 jellybean-sized eggs. • Ruby-throats winter in Central America, with many flying 800 km non-stop over the Gulf of Mexico. **Where found:** open, mixed woodlands, wetlands, gardens, backyards; uncommon in central and southern areas, May–Aug.

Belted Kingfisher

Megaceryle alcyon

Length: 28–36 cm
Wingspan: 51 cm

Chronically antisocial other than during the brief nesting period, kingfishers stake out productive fishing grounds and scold invaders with loud rattling calls. They catch fish with headfirst plunges, and often beat the victim into submission by rapping it against a branch. • Mating pairs nest in a chamber at the end of a long tunnel dug into an earth bank. • With a red band across her belly, the female kingfisher is more colourful than her mate. **Where found:** lakes, ponds, rivers; fairly common, but rare in grasslands, Apr–Oct.

Downy Woodpecker

Picoides pubescens

Length: 15–18 cm
Wingspan: 30 cm

Easily our most common woodpecker, the downy is found everywhere from backyard feeders to dense forest. It closely resembles the less common hairy woodpecker (*P. villosus*) but is much smaller, with a proportionately tiny bill and black spots on the white outer tail feathers.
• Downies and other woodpeckers have feathered nostrils that filter out sawdust produced by their excavations, and long barbed tongues that can reach far into crevices to extract grubs and other morsels. **Where found:** deciduous and mixed forests; common year-round resident wherever there are woodlands.

Northern Flicker

Colaptes auratus

Length: 32–33 cm
Wingspan: 51 cm

The northern flicker spends much of its time on the ground, feeding on ants. Flickers also clean themselves by squashing ants and preening themselves with the remains. Ants contain formic acid, which kills small parasites on the birds' skin and feathers. • When these woodpeckers fly, they reveal a bold white rump and colourful underwings. Our eastern birds, with their yellow underwings, are "yellowshafted flickers"; western birds have salmon-coloured underwings and are "redshafted flickers." **Where found:** open woodlands, forest edges, fields, wetlands, treed suburbia; common Apr–Oct, uncommon and local on prairie Nov–Mar.

Pileated Woodpecker

Dryocopus pileatus

Length: 41–48 cm
Wingspan: 74 cm

This crow-sized bird, the 6th-largest woodpecker in the world, is an unforgettable sight. Its loud, maniacal laughing calls give it away, but seeing this secretive woodpecker is more difficult. Its large, distinctively oval-shaped nest hole also reveals its presence, as do trees that look as if someone had taken an axe to them. The pileated feeds heavily on carpenter ants, and that's what it is digging for. Wood ducks, American kestrels, owls and even flying squirrels nest in abandoned pileated woodpecker nest holes. **Where found:** large, mature forests; fairly common to uncommon year-round in boreal forest, aspen parkland.

Least Flycatcher

Empidonax minimus

Length: 13–15 cm
Wingspan: 20 cm

The least flycatcher introduces the largest order of birds—the Passeriformes—usually known as passerines, songbirds or perching birds. • Perfectly camouflaged, least flycatchers have olive brown plumage, white eye rings and 2 white wing bars. In spring, courting males issue a loud, 2-part *che-bek* call throughout much of the day. Vocalizations are key to identifying flycatcher species. • Flycatchers sally from exposed perches to snatch flying insects in midair, a foraging behaviour known as flycatching or hawking, among others. **Where found:** open deciduous or mixed woodlands, forest openings and edges; absent from northern areas, common to abundant elsewhere, May–Sept.

Eastern Phoebe

Sayornis phoebe

Length: 15–18 cm
Wingspan: 27 cm

Phoebes often build their mud nest on building ledges, the eaves of barns and sheds, and bridge trestles; consequently, they are close to people. They utter loud, emphatic *fee-bee!* notes and are known for their tail-wagging behaviour. • Phoebes are among the earliest flycatchers to return in spring, and they immediately begin nest building. With such an early start, phoebe pairs regularly raise 2 broods during the nesting season, often reusing the same nest. **Where found:** open deciduous woodlands, forest edges and clearings, often near water; central SK/MB, Apr–Sept.

Eastern Kingbird

Tyrannus tyrannus

Length: 22 cm
Wingspan: 38 cm

The eastern kingbird lives up to its scientific name, *Tyrannus tyrannus.* It will fearlessly attack crows, hawks and even humans that pass through its territory, pursuing and pecking at them until the threat has passed. It is a bird of very open landscapes, and often perches prominently on roadside wires. • The eastern kingbird is a gregarious fruit eater while wintering in South America, and an antisocial, aggressive insect eater while nesting in North America. **Where found:** fields, agricultural landscapes with scattered trees, large forest clearings, shrubby roadsides, borders of marshes, treed suburbia; central and southern SK/MB, May–Aug.

Northern Shrike

Lanius excubitor

Length: 25 cm
Wingspan: 37 cm

Shrikes are predatory birds that kill and eat small birds
or rodents, swooping down on them from above.
Northern shrikes lack powerful talons and rely on
their sharp, hooked bills to catch prey. Males
display their hunting competence to females by impaling their prey on thorns or
barbed wire (which may also be a means of storing excess food). • The similar
loggerhead shrike *(L. ludovicianus)* is a fairly common summer resident in the
grasslands, but the species have little seasonal overlap. **Where found:** uncommon
breeder in northern taiga regions May–Sept, uncommon and erratic in open
country, farmyards, towns, roadsides during migration and winter, Oct–Apr.

Red-eyed Vireo

Vireo olivaceus

Length: 15 cm
Wingspan: 25 cm

Capable of delivering about 40 phrases per minute, male
red-eyed vireos monotonously drone on all day. A patient
researcher once tallied 22,000 individual songs delivered
by one of these avian motormouths in a single day. Such
incessant yammering earned these birds the nick-
name "preacher birds." • Although a "can't miss" in
the hearing department, the red-eyed vireo is hard
to spot because it sluggishly forages high in the canopy, hidden in dense leafy cover.
Where found: deciduous or mixed woodlands; common to abundant throughout
during summer and migration, except in northern reaches.

Gray Jay

Perisoreus canadensis

Length: 28–33 cm
Wingspan: 46 cm

Few birds exceed mischievous gray jays for curiosity and
boldness. Attracted by any foreign sound or potential feeding opportunity, small family groups glide gently and
unexpectedly out of spruce stands to introduce themselves
to any passersby. These intelligent birds are known to
hide bits of food under the bark of trees, to be
retrieved in times of need. • Gray jays nest earlier than other songbirds in our region,
laying their eggs in late February. The young regularly fledge before the snow melts.
Where found: coniferous forests; uncommon in north, common in central parts,
rare in south, year-round. **Also known as:** Canada jay, whiskey jack, camp robber.

Blue Jay

Cyanocitta cristata

Length: 28–31 cm
Wingspan: 41 cm

This loud, striking, well-known bird can be quite aggressive when competing for sunflower seeds and peanuts at backyard feeders. It rarely hesitates to drive away smaller birds, squirrels or even cats. • This jay prolifically caches nuts and is important to the forest ecosystem. In autumn, a blue jay might bury several thousand acorns, forgetting where most were hidden and thus planting many oak trees. **Where found:** habitat generalist, from dense forests to suburbia; common in boreal forest and aspen parkland, rare and local in south, year-round.

Black-billed Magpie

Pica hudsonia

Length: 46 cm
Wingspan: 64 cm

It is hard to imagine southern Saskatchewan and Manitoba without these beautiful, long-tailed chatterboxes, but magpies withdrew from our provinces during the time of the great bison slaughters. They soon returned to recolonize southern regions, cleverly adapting to life in both rural and urban areas. • These exceptional architects construct large, domed stick nests that conceal and protect eggs and young from harsh weather and predators. Abandoned nests remain in trees for years and are often reused by other birds. **Where found:** farmyards, hedgerows, open groves, suburbia; central and southern SK/MB, year-round.

American Crow

Corvus brachyrhynchos

Length: 43–53 cm
Wingspan: 94 cm

One of our most intelligent birds, the crow has in recent years occupied urban places in much greater numbers. It knows it is safe from hunters—the crow is legal game in many areas—and towns offer this opportunistic scavenger abundant food. • Crows will drop walnuts or clams from great heights onto a hard surface to crack the shells, one of the few examples of birds using objects to manipulate food. • Very social, crows sometimes form massive winter roosts that can number into the thousands. **Where found:** nearly ubiquitous; urban areas, agricultural fields, forests; uncommon in north, common to abundant elsewhere, Mar–Oct but a few may overwinter.

Common Raven

Corvus corax

Length: 61 cm
Wingspan: 1.3 m

Glorified in native cultures throughout the Northern Hemisphere, the raven has earned a reputation as a crafty, clever bird. This adaptable, widespread bird uses its wits to survive along coastlines, in deserts, in temperate regions, on arctic tundra and in suburbia. The raven produces complex vocalizations, forms lifelong pair bonds and exhibits problem-solving skills. When working as a pair to confiscate a meal, one raven may act as the decoy while the other steals the food. **Where found:** nearly ubiquitous; urban areas, forests, landfills; boreal forest and northward year-round, southern SK/MB Oct–Mar.

Horned Lark

Eremophila alpestris

Length: 18 cm
Wingspan: 30 cm

Seemingly nondescript, horned larks scurry like mice across the most barren landscapes. They often flush from rural roadsides as cars pass by; watch for the blackish tail that contrasts with the sandy-coloured body. A good look at perched larks reveals a black mask, twin tiny "horns" and pale yellow underparts smudged with a dark crescent across the chest. Listen for their clear, tinkling calls in open agricultural lands. **Where found:** open areas, pastures, prairie, cultivated fields; common migrant in boreal plains and northward Apr and Oct, common on prairie Mar–Oct, uncommon in settled, southern areas Nov–Mar.

Tree Swallow

Tachycineta bicolor

Length: 14 cm
Wingspan: 37 cm

The first tree swallows return to our region in late April. Competition for cavity nest sites is fierce, and the swallows that arrive the earliest are the most likely to secure good cavity nests. Bluebird enthusiasts have greatly helped this cavity-nesting species, because tree swallows readily adopt bluebird boxes. • When the hunting is good, these busy birds are known to return to their young 10 to 20 times per hour. **Where found:** often seen in areas with bluebird nest boxes; open habitats with peak numbers around ponds, lakes, wetlands; common throughout, May–Aug.

Barn Swallow

Hirundo rustica

Length: 18 cm
Wingspan: 38 cm

Barn swallows are familiar sights under bridges and picnic shelters or around farmsteads, where they nest in barns and other buildings. It is now almost unheard of for them to nest in natural sites such as cliffs, to which they once were restricted. Their nests are constructed by rolling mud into small balls, one mouthful of mud at a time. • In males, the long forked tail is a sign of vigour; longer-tailed males tend to live longer and have higher reproductive success. **Where found:** open landscapes, especially rural and agricultural, often near water; common on prairie, uncommon and local elsewhere, May–Sept.

Black-capped Chickadee

Poecile atricapillus

Length: 13–15 cm
Wingspan: 20 cm

Curious and inquisitive, black-capped chickadees have been known to land on people. They are very common and familiar visitors to backyard feeders. Chickadees cache seeds and are able to relocate hidden food up to a month later.
• Chickadees are omnivorous cavity nesters that usually lay 6 to 8 eggs in late winter or early spring. • On cold winter nights, chickadees may huddle together in the shelter of tree cavities or other suitable hollows. **Where found:** mixed and deciduous forests, parks, suburban backyards; absent from extreme north, rare in grasslands, common elsewhere, year-round.

Red-breasted Nuthatch

Sitta canadensis

Length: 11 cm
Wingspan: 22 cm

The red-breasted nuthatch moves down tree trunks headfirst, searching for bark-dwelling insects. Red-breasted nuthatches stage periodic southward invasions some winters, which are termed irruptions. Thus, they may be absent at feeders some winters and common the next. Irruptions are triggered by food shortages, not weather. Nuthatches are especially attracted to backyard feeders filled with suet or peanut butter. **Where found:** coniferous and mixed forests; uncommon to fairly common in aspen parkland, boreal forest and Cypress Hills year-round, fairly common migrant on southern prairie Apr–May and Oct.

House Wren

Troglodytes aedon

Length: 12 cm
Wingspan: 15 cm

A familiar suburban sight and sound, the house wren has a loud, bubbly warble. It typically skulks in dense brush but won't hesitate to express its displeasure with intruders by delivering harsh, scolding notes. • The house wren can be aggressive and highly territorial and is known to puncture the eggs of other birds that nest nearby. This cavity nester is easily lured to nest boxes. • This wren ranges all the way from Canada to southern South America—the broadest longitudinal distribution of any wren. **Where found:** thickets, shrubby openings, woodland openings, often near buildings; common in suburban prairie areas, uncommon and local elsewhere, May–Sept.

Mountain Bluebird

Sialia currucoides

Length: 18 cm
Wingspan: 36 cm

Bluebird enthusiasts have erected thousands of nest boxes throughout the range of this cavity-nesting thrush, greatly bolstering populations. Natural nest sites, such as woodpecker cavities or holes in sandstone cliffs, are in high demand as a result of habitat loss and increased competition with aggressive, introduced European Starlings. • Male mountain bluebirds are a brilliant sky blue, and females are duller. Eastern bluebirds *(S. sialis)* are found in southeastern Saskatchewan and southern Manitoba; males are deep blue above and warm rufous below. **Where found:** common on prairie, uncommon, local elsewhere, Apr–Sept.

American Robin

Turdus migratorius

Length: 25 cm
Wingspan: 43 cm

Flocks of American robins arrive in March to welcome spring with their cheery songs. Among our most widely seen, familiar and easily recognized birds, robins occur nearly everywhere. Striking males have black heads, rich brick-red underparts and streaked white throats. • Robins are master earthworm-hunters, adeptly spotting a worm and tugging it from the soil. In winter, they switch to a diet of berries. **Where found:** habitat generalist; residential lawns, gardens, urban parks, forests, bogs; fairly common in north, abundant in south, Mar–Nov but may overwinter near fruit-bearing trees and springs.

Gray Catbird

Dumetella carolinensis

Length: 22–23 cm
Wingspan: 28 cm

A catbird in full song issues a non-stop, squeaky barrage of warbling notes, interspersed with poor imitations of other birds. Occasionally it lets go with loud, cat-like meows that could even fool a feline. This bird occupies thick brushy habitats and can be difficult to glimpse, but squeaking sounds may lure it into view. Perseverance pays off; this handsome bird displays tones of grey set off by a dark cap and striking cinnamon undertail coverts. **Where found:** dense thickets, brambles or shrubby areas, hedgerows, often near water; common in central and southern areas, May–Sept.

Brown Thrasher

Toxostoma rufum

Length: 29 cm
Wingspan: 33 cm

Looking somewhat thrush-like with their rufous
backs and spotted underparts, brown thrashers are
mimics. Thrashers have the most expansive repertoire
of all North American birds; some 3000 distinct phrases have been catalogued.
Singing thrashers often deliver their songs from near the tip of a small tree.
Thrashers nest close to the ground and must defend their nests against snakes and
other nest robbers. **Where found:** open areas interspersed with fencerows, dense
thickets, dry brushy fields, woodland edges; uncommon in central areas, common
in south, May–Sept but a few may overwinter.

European Starling

Sturnus vulgaris

Length: 22 cm
Wingspan: 41 cm

We can thank the Shakespeare Society for this
species, which is perhaps the most damaging
non-native bird introduced in North America.
About 60 European starlings were released in New York City in
1890 and 1891 as part of an ill-fated effort to release into the U.S. all the birds
mentioned in Shakespeare's works. Now abundant throughout North America,
long-lived starlings often drive native species such as bluebirds from nest cavities.
Where found: cities, towns, farmyards, woodland fringes, clearings; uncommon and
local in north, common to abundant in central and southern parts, Apr–Oct, uncommon at farmsteads and in cities during winter.

Bohemian Waxwing

Bombycilla garrulus

Length: 18 cm
Wingspan: 30 cm

With its black mask and slick hairdo, the bohemian waxwing
has a suave look. • Waxwings are most noticeable in winter,
when large, nomadic flocks plunder the fruit of mountain
ash trees and various berry bushes, sometimes getting
tipsy on fermented fruit. Although largely frugivorous
(fruit eating), waxwings also flycatch in summer, often
near water. • In spring, when bohemian waxwings fly north to
nest, they are replaced by cedar waxwings (*B. cedrorum*). **Where found:** fairly
common in northern forests, riparian areas, farm shelterbelts, wooded residential
parks, gardens Mar–Nov, uncommon to abundant on prairie Nov–Mar.

Yellow Warbler

Dendroica petechia

Length: 13 cm
Wingspan: 20 cm

Warblers are among our most beautiful birds, and the yellow warbler is one of our showiest. It sings a loud, ringing *sweet-sweet-I'm-so-sweet* song. • This warbler is often parasitized by the brown-headed cowbird and has learned to recognize cowbird eggs. But instead of tossing the foreign eggs out, the yellow warbler will build another nest overtop the old eggs or abandon the nest completely. Occasionally, cowbirds strike repeatedly—a 5-storey nest was once found! **Where found:** habitat generalist; moist, open woodlands, scrubby meadows, urban parks and gardens; common throughout, May–Aug.

Yellow-rumped Warbler

Dendroica coronata

Length: 13–15 cm
Wingspan: 23 cm

Yellow-rumped warblers are the most abundant and widespread wood-warblers in North America. There are 2 races of the yellow-rumped warbler, the "Myrtle warbler," which has a white throat, and the "Audubon's warbler," which has a yellow throat. Both occur in our region. The "Myrtle" is the dominant race, except for in the Cypress Hills, which is the summer home of the "Audubon's" race. **Where found:** mature coniferous and mixed woodlands; boreal plain and boreal forest May–Sept, migrant on prairie May and late Aug–Sept.

American Redstart

Setophaga ruticilla

Length: 13 cm
Wingspan: 21 cm

The hyperactive American redstart compulsively flicks its wings and fans its tail. It is thought that by flashing the bright orange or yellow spots in their plumage, the bird flushes insects from the foliage. A broad bill and rictal bristles (the short, whisker-like feathers around its mouth) help it capture insects like a flycatcher. Females and first-year males have yellow marks instead of orange, so if a "yellowstart" is seen singing, it is a young male. **Where found:** dense shrubby understorey of deciduous woodlands, often near water; central SK/MB May–Aug, migrant on prairie May and mid-Aug–Sept.

Common Yellowthroat

Geothlypis trichas

Length: 11–14 cm
Wingspan: 18 cm

The little masked bandit's loud *witchity witchity witchity* song bursting from the cattails gives away this skulker. The common yellowthroat is probably our most common breeding warbler, reaching peak numbers in wetlands and damp overgrown fields. It has wren-like curiosity, and you can coax it into view by making squeaking or "pishing" sounds. The female can be confusing to identify but shares the male's odd big-headed, slender-bodied, long-legged dimensions. **Where found:** wetlands, riparian areas, wet, overgrown meadows; central and southern SK/MB, May–Sept.

Eastern and Spotted Towhee

Pipilo spp.

Length: 18–21 cm
Wingspan: 26 cm

Towhees are large, colourful, chunky sparrows with long tails. These noisy birds are often heard before they are seen as they rustle about in dense undergrowth. They employ an unusual 2-footed shuffling technique to uncover food items. • In 1995, the rufous-sided towhee was split into 2 species. The spotted towhee occurs from Saskatchewan west and sings several hurried notes followed by a buzzy trill: *che che che che che zheee!* The eastern towhee occurs from Manitoba east and sings a loud whistled *drink your teeee.* **Where found:** open woods, brushy fields, woodland borders, overgrown gardens, parks; southern SK/MB, May–Sept.

Chipping Sparrow

Spizella passerina

Length: 13–15 cm
Wingspan: 22 cm

The chipping sparrow can be distinguished from other sparrows by its rufous crown and prominent white "eyebrow." This bird's trilling song, however, is very similar to that of the dark-eyed junco. Listen for the chipping sparrow's rapid trill, which is slightly faster, drier and less musical. • In southern parts of Saskatchewan and Manitoba, chipping sparrows are generally restricted to cities, towns and farmsteads, and they are particularly drawn to conifers. **Where found:** open coniferous or mixed woodland edges, shrubby yards, gardens; throughout, May–Sept.

107

White-throated Sparrow

Zonotrichia albicollis

Length: 17–18 cm
Wingspan: 23 cm

White-throated sparrows sing in a distinctive, somewhat mournful minor key: a clear whistled *dear sweet Canada Canada Canada,* very characteristic of boreal forests. • Unique among sparrows, this species has 2 colour morphs: one has black and white stripes on the head, and the other has brown and tan stripes. So, a duller tan-coloured bird is not necessarily a female, nor is a bright white-striped bird always a male. **Where found:** coniferous and mixed forests; boreal plain northward May–Oct, migrant on prairie May and Sept–Oct.

Dark-eyed Junco

Junco hyemalis

Length: 14–17 cm
Wingspan: 23 cm

Juncos are one of North America's most abundant songbirds, with a total population estimated at 630 million birds. When flushed, dark-eyed juncos flash prominent white outer tail feathers. These feathers may serve as "lures" for raptors; a pursuing hawk fixates on the white flashes and will grab only a few tail feathers, enabling the junco to escape. **Where found:** coniferous and mixedwood forests; boreal plain northward Apr–Oct, prairie Apr–May and Sept–Oct, uncommon in central and southern areas Nov–Mar, mainly at feeders or granaries.

Rose-breasted Grosbeak

Pheucticus ludovicianus

Length: 18–21 cm
Wingspan: 32 cm

The rose-breasted grosbeak sounds like a robin that has taken singing lessons. Its call note is a squeaky sound reminiscent of a sneaker on a basketball court. Listening for the grosbeak is a good way to find it—it remains high in leafy canopies and is rather sluggish. • Males have beautiful black-and-white plumage and a bold, inverted "V" of crimson-pink on the breast. Females are muted and resemble big sparrows, but are unusual for songbirds in that they also sing. **Where found:** deciduous and mixed forests; boreal plain June–Aug, prairie migrant May and Aug.

Red-winged Blackbird

Agelaius phoeniceus

Length: 18–24 cm
Wingspan: 33 cm

Red-winged blackbirds are one of North America's most abundant birds. Males are stunning, and when they court females by thrusting their wings forward to flare the brilliant scarlet-orange epaulets, they appear as grand as any of our birds. • Males are avian polygamists that may have 15 females in their territory. • True harbingers of spring, they make loud, raspy *konk-a-ree* calls that can be heard in early April. **Where found:** cattail marshes, wet meadows, ditches, agricultural areas, overgrown fields; rare in north, common to abundant elsewhere, Apr–Oct but a few may overwinter in south.

Western Meadowlark

Sturnella neglecta

Length: 24 cm
Wingspan: 40 cm

This bird's clear, ringing, whistled songs are characteristic sounds of grasslands and fields. • From above, meadowlarks are muted in sombre hues of speckled brown, allowing them to blend with the vegetation. Seen from below, their striking, lemon-yellow breast is struck across with a bold, black chevron. When flushed, meadowlarks reveal conspicuous, white outer tail feathers, and they fly with distinctive stiff, shallow wingbeats. **Where found:** grassy meadows, roadsides, pastures, agricultural areas; uncommon and local in central areas, common in prairie ecozone, Apr–Oct.

Yellow-headed Blackbird

Xanthocephalus xanthocephalus

Length: 23–28 cm
Wingspan: 35–38 cm

You might be taken aback by the pitiful grinding sound produced when the male yellow-headed blackbird perches on a cattail stalk and arches his dazzling golden head backward to "sing" a nonmuscial series of grating notes. • Where yellow-headed blackbirds occur with red-winged blackbirds, the larger yellow-heads dominate, pushing their red-winged competitors to the periphery, where predation is highest. **Where found:** permanent marshes, sloughs, lakeshores, river impoundments with emergent vegetation, fields; common in prairie ecozone, uncommon in central reaches, Apr–Oct but a few may overwinter.

Brown-headed Cowbird

Molothrus ater

Length: 15–20 cm
Wingspan: 30 cm

Cowbirds are reviled as nest parasites: they lay their eggs in other birds' nests and are known to parasitize more than 140 bird species. Upon hatching, baby cowbirds out-compete the host's young, leading to nest failure. This strange habit evolved with the birds' association with nomadic bison herds. As the animals moved about, cowbirds were not in one place long enough to tend their own nests. Even though bison no longer occur here, cowbirds haven't forgotten their roots and still commonly forage around cattle. **Where found:** agricultural and residential areas, woodland edges, now nearly ubiquitous; central and southern SK/MB, May–Aug.

Baltimore Oriole

Icterus galbula

Length: 18–20 cm
Wingspan: 29 cm

The clear, flute-like whistles of this tropical blackbird are common sounds where large trees are found, even in suburbia. Even a crude whistled imitation can send the male oriole rocketing down to investigate. • Baltimore orioles make interesting hanging, pouch-like nests woven of plant fibres, which become conspicuous once the leaves have fallen. Formerly associated with mature elm trees, orioles have shifted preference to cottonwoods in areas where Dutch elm disease has eliminated elms. **Where found:** open deciduous and mixed forests, particularly riparian woodlands; common on prairie, fairly common but local in central parts, May–Aug.

Purple Finch

Carpodacus purpureus

Length: 13–15 cm
Wingspan: 25 cm

Male purple finches are more raspberry red than purple. The male finch often delivers his musical, warble from an exposed perch at the top of a live tree. • Purple finches are particularly attracted to sunflower seeds, and small flocks can be lured to southern feeders in winter. However, they are cyclically irruptive; during some winters many more move south than in other years. **Where found:** coniferous and mixed forests; boreal plain Apr–Oct, prairie migrant Apr–May and Sept–Oct, occasionally overwinters in south.

Common Redpoll

Carduelis flammea

Length: 13 cm
Wingspan: 23 cm

Redpolls sometimes make only a modest appearance, showing up in winter in small groups. Other winters, dozens flock together, gleaning waste grain from bare fields or stocking up at winter feeders. • A large surface area relative to a small internal volume puts the common redpoll at risk of freezing in low temperatures. A high intake of food and the insulating layer of warm air trapped by its fluffed feathers keep this songbird from dying of hypothermia. **Where found:** fairly common in northern areas year-round, irruptive and uncommon to abundant in weedy fields, roadsides, backyard feeders elsewhere Nov–May.

American Goldfinch

Carduelis tristis

Length: 11–14 cm
Wingspan: 23 cm

Vibrant American goldfinches utter a jubilant *po-ta-to-chip* call and fly with a distinctive, undulating flight style. Commonly seen in weedy fields, gardens and along roadsides, these acrobatic birds regularly feed while hanging upside down. Finch feeders are designed with the seed openings below the perches to discourage the more aggressive, upright-feeding birds. Use niger or black-oil sunflower seeds to attract American goldfinches to your bird feeder. **Where found:** weedy fields, riparian areas, parks, gardens; central and southern regions, May–Sept.

House Sparrow

Passer domesticus

Length: 14–17 cm
Wingspan: 24 cm

A black mask and bib adorn the male of this adaptive, aggressive species. • This abundant and conspicuous bird was introduced to North America in the 1850s as part of a plan to control the insects that were damaging grain and cereal crops. As it turns out, this species is largely vegetarian and usually feeds on seeds and grain! It also frequents fast-food restaurant parking lots, backyard bird feeders and farms. **Where found:** any human environment; abundant on prairie, uncommon and local elsewhere, year-round.

AMPHIBIANS & REPTILES

A mphibians and reptiles are commonly referred to as cold blooded, but this term is misleading. Although reptiles and amphibians lack the ability to generate internal body heat, they are not necessarily cold blooded. These animals are ectothermic or poikilothermic, meaning that the temperature of the surrounding environment governs their body temperature. The animal will obtain heat from sunlight, warm rocks and logs, and warmed earth. Amphibians and reptiles hibernate in winter in cold regions, and some species of reptiles estivate (are dormant during hot or dry periods) in summer in hot regions. Both amphibians and reptiles moult (shed their skins) as they grow to larger body sizes.

Amphibians are smooth skinned and most live in moist habitats. They are represented by the salamanders, toads and frogs. These species typically lay shell-less eggs in jelly-like masses in water. The eggs hatch into gilled larvae, which later metamorphose into adults with lungs and legs. Amphibians can regenerate their skin and sometimes even entire limbs. Male and female amphibians often differ in size and colour, and males may have other specialized features when sexually mature, such as the vocal sacs in many frogs and toads.

Reptiles are completely terrestrial vertebrates with scaly skin. In this guide, the representatives are turtles, lizards and snakes. Most reptiles lay eggs buried in loose soil, but some snakes and lizards give birth to live young. Reptiles do not have a larval stage.

Salamanders
p. 113

Toads & Frogs
pp. 114–16

Turtles
p. 117

Lizards
p. 118

Snakes
pp. 118–20

Mudpuppy

Necturus maculosus

Length: 48 cm

These huge salamanders inhabit deep, muddy water and are largely nocturnal; thus they are seldom seen. Unlike other salamanders, mudpuppies keep their feathery external gills throughout their adult lives. These bottom-dwellers spend much of their time eating aquatic insects, crayfish and small fish or hiding under debris on the bottom of lakes and streams. **Where found:** river and lake bottoms; southeastern MB.

Blue-spotted Salamander

Ambystoma laterale

Length: up to 12 cm

The blue-spotted salamander is a striking creature; its glossy black skin is heavily flecked with porcelain blue spots. • Salamanders live most of their life underground or beneath leaf litter. The best time to see them is on a rainy spring night, when groups gather in clear, shallow ponds to breed. Females attach jelly-like clumps of eggs to underwater vegetation. **Where found:** moist, deciduous forests near fish-free wetlands; hibernates underground; southeastern MB.

Tiger Salamander

Ambystoma tigrinum

Length: up to 40 cm

These whoppers can reach 40 cm in length and resemble mini komodo dragons as they swagger along. Tiger salamanders are richly patterned in dull yellow blotches that contrast with their greyish black ground colour. They prefer more open landscapes than other mole salamanders and are often found far from woods or water during early spring migrations. They lay their eggs in shallow pools and even farm ponds, but will vanish if fish are introduced. Most salamanders require fishless ponds—fish are voracious predators that quickly consume amphibian eggs and young. **Where found:** farms, prairie, wet woods near water; hibernates underground; southern half of SK, southwestern MB.

Plains Spadefoot Toad

Spea bombifrons

Length: 6 cm

The spadefoot is named for the pointed, dark-edged "spade" on its hind foot that it uses for digging. The toad tunnels backward into loose, sandy soil to make an underground burrow that allows it to take shelter and conserve moisture in dry habitats. Burrows as deep as 1 m underground have been found. • The plains spadefoot's call is similar to the harsh barks of a wood frog. It breeds in temporary ponds that form after spring rain showers. **Where found:** sandy or gravelly soils in short-grass prairie; rare to uncommon in southern SK and southwestern MB.

American Toad

Bufo americanus

Length: 11 cm

One of spring's great amphibian spectacles is the mass chorus of trilling American toads. For about a month, these warty songsters deliver loud, lengthy, monotonous but semi-musical trills from almost any patch of water. Left in their wake are long strings of egg masses that soon hatch tiny black tadpoles. • Toads have parotoid glands behind the eyes that contain a toxin that can sicken predators. **Where found:** various habitats, including forests, meadows, suburban backyards, gardens; hibernates under soil; central and eastern MB.

Canadian Toad

Bufo hemiophrys

Length: *Male:* 7 cm; *Female:* 8 cm

Listen for the Canadian toad's short, harsh trill in spring. This small brown, grey or greenish toad is covered with warts and has a distinctive hump, called a boss, between its protruding eyes. • The Canadian and similar-looking American toads' ranges overlap in central Manitoba, but from there, Canadian toads occur to the west and American toads are found to the east. **Where found:** prairie, aspen parkland, boreal forest ponds; hibernates underground; central and western MB, most of SK.

Grey Treefrog

Hyla versicolor

Length: 6 cm

Many people who have heard this diminutive tree dweller probably thought the sound came from a bird. Quite arboreal, grey tree-frogs frequently deliver a loud, rather coarse trill from high in the foliage that carries some distance. • Grey treefrogs can change colour like chameleons to perfectly match their background; they can morph between a rather bright grey-green to dull pearly grey. Tiny suction-cup grippers on their toes allow for Spiderman-like climbing ability. • Treefrogs breed in weedy ponds, depositing clumps of floating eggs. **Where found:** woodlands near water; hibernates under soil or leaves; southern MB.

Spring Peeper

Pseudacris crucifer

Length: 3.5 cm

A distinctive sound of early spring is the loud, bird-like peeps of this tiny frog. It is amazing how loud their calls are; stand-ing amidst a pack of peepers chorusing in a wetland will almost cause your ears to hurt. Spring peepers begin calling and mating as soon as ice thaws from ponds and wetlands, and they are only conspicuous at this time. For much of the rest of the year, they forage in low shrubs and leaf litter and are much less likely to be detected. Peepers are easily identified by the dark, X-shaped mark on their tan to grey backs. **Where found:** forest floors near water; hibernates under leaf litter; central and eastern MB.

Boreal Chorus Frog

Pseudacris maculata

Length: 3 cm

In early spring, you can hear the chorus frog calling from wetlands, often along with the *cluck cluck* of wood frogs. The chorus frog's commonly heard sound resembles the sound made by running a finger down the teeth of a comb—but projected through a stack of Marshall amps. • This tiny frog has a grey-brown body, a dark eye stripe and 3 darker, sometimes broken, stripes running along its back. **Where found:** breeds in ponds, marshes, ephemeral water bodies; hibernates under leaf litter; throughout except northern reaches.

Northern Leopard Frog

Rana pipiens

Length: *Male:* 8 cm; *Female:* 10 cm

The leopard frog is often seen when flushed from grass in wet meadows or near wetlands. But you won't see much—just a froggy blur shooting off in huge, zigzagging bounds. With a bit of patience, the leaper can usually be tracked down and admired. • It's easy to see where the name comes from: these frogs are patterned with very distinctive leopard-like spots. They are often heard, too, but it's likely that most people don't recognize the calls as those of a frog. They emit a curious, low snoring sound, sometimes even delivered under water. **Where found:** meadows, fields, marshes during summer; hibernates on lake bottoms; throughout except northern areas.

Wood Frog

Rana sylvatica

Length: 4.5 cm

Wood frogs are amphibians with antifreeze. At below-zero temperatures, their heart rate, blood flow and breathing stop, turning them into froggy ice cubes. Special compounds, mainly glucose, allow them to survive partial freezing and thawing of their tissues. Thus, they are able to range north of the Arctic Circle, farther north than any other amphibian. • In early spring, when ice still fringes woodland pools, vernal wetlands explode to life as wood frogs invade to mate and lay eggs. Their collective calls sound like distant ducks quacking. **Where found:** moist woodlands, sometimes far from water; throughout except extreme southern SK.

Common Snapping Turtle

Chelydra serpentina

Length: 45 cm

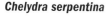

Mess with one of
these prehistoric-
looking beasts when
it's on land and you'll
quickly learn how it
got its name. When threatened, the
hostile turtle lunges its neck out a surprising distance and snaps menacingly with
powerful jaws. Tales of them snapping broom-
sticks are greatly exaggerated but snappers can
inflict a nasty bite. • This turtle spends most of its time underwater, walking along
lake or pond bottoms eating weeds and scavenging for carrion. In early summer,
females emerge on land to seek sites to bury their white, spherical eggs (our other
turtles lay oval eggs). **Where found:** lakes, ponds, marshes; southern SK/MB.

Western Painted Turtle

Chrysemys picta belli

Length: 25 cm

Painted turtles
can be seen basking
in the sun on top of floating logs, mats
of vegetation or exposed rocks. When alarmed, they slip into the water for a quick
escape. • These turtles may live for up to 40 years. • There are 3 painted turtle
subspecies, but only the largest, the western painted turtle, is found in our region.
It has an olive green carapace with red or orange underside borders. **Where
found:** marshes, ponds, lakes, slow-flowing streams; southern SK, central MB.

Greater Short-horned Lizard

Phrynosoma hernandesi

Length: *Male:* 5 cm;
Female: 7 cm

Short, flat and horny, these small lizards typically bask on warm, south-facing slopes and wait for a meal to pass by. Ants, especially native red ones, are preferred prey. • These well-camouflaged creatures emerge from their shallow winter burrows and mate in late May. Females give birth to live young, unlike most lizards, which lay eggs. • These lizards reach the northern limit of their range in southern Saskatchewan. Agriculture and oil and gas activities are main threats to this species. **Where found:** mixed-grass prairie with vegetative cover such as sagebrush; patchy distribution near the South Saskatchewan and Milk rivers of southern SK; endangered.

Smooth Greensnake

Opheodrys vernalis

Length: 65 cm

The smooth greensnake is so beautiful and gentle that even a person with ophidiophobia (fear of snakes) might not mind it. It is painted in exquisite hues of emerald, often washed with a pale lemon colour below, and it will not bite even when picked up. • Smooth greensnakes' extraordinary colour allows them to blend well with the grasses in which they forage. Road-killed snakes stand out—they quickly turn blue upon death. • A number of females may share a single nesting site, where each female lays 3 to 12 eggs under rocks, in loose soil. Groups sometimes hibernate in anthills. **Where found:** moist meadows, grasslands, prairie; southern SK/MB.

Red-bellied Snake

Storeria occipitomaculata

Length: 40 cm

Distinguished by a red to pink coloured belly and keeled scales, this snake is easy to identify but may be hard to find. The red-bellied snake usually remains hidden under fallen logs, rocks or leaf litter. Your best chance of meeting one is at night on a rainy or overcast day, when it emerges to feed on small invertebrates, especially slugs. Females bear up 12 live young in autumn. During winter, groups hibernate in a den. **Where found:** forest floor, under cover; southern SK/MB.

Red-sided Gartersnake

Thamnophis sirtalis parietalis

Length: 60 cm
(maximum 1 m)

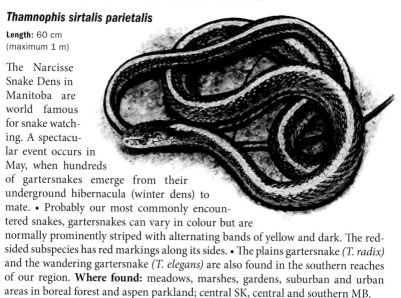

The Narcisse Snake Dens in Manitoba are world famous for snake watching. A spectacular event occurs in May, when hundreds of gartersnakes emerge from their underground hibernacula (winter dens) to mate. • Probably our most commonly encountered snakes, gartersnakes can vary in colour but are normally prominently striped with alternating bands of yellow and dark. The red-sided subspecies has red markings along its sides. • The plains gartersnake *(T. radix)* and the wandering gartersnake *(T. elegans)* are also found in the southern reaches of our region. **Where found:** meadows, marshes, gardens, suburban and urban areas in boreal forest and aspen parkland; central SK, central and southern MB.

Western Hog-nosed Snake

Heterodon nasicus

Length: up to 95 cm

An extraordinary actor, the western hog-nosed snake is a master of the bluff. If threatened, it will hiss and expand its neck, giving it the look of a cobra. If this response fails to frighten, it will flip over and play dead, even lolling its tongue out the side of its mouth for effect. • This snake favours sandy or gravelly soil and uses its upturned snout to dig for toads, frogs or salamanders to prey upon. • It has large, dark blotches on a lighter background and a distinctly upturned snout. **Where found:** sandy soil or gravelly areas adjacent to prairie, scrublands or floodplains; southern SK, extreme southwestern MB; widely distributed but may be declining.

Prairie Rattlesnake

Crotalus viridis

Length: up to 1.5 m

Our only venomous snake, the prairie rattlesnake warns away intruders by shaking the rattle at the tip of its tail. Those that ignore the warning risk a poisonous bite. A rattlesnake's deadly fangs are hinged and can be folded back into the mouth. • Prairie rattlesnakes are light brown and blotched overall, with a triangular head, vertical pupils and special heat-sensing facial pits for locating warm-blooded prey. • During winter, rattlesnakes den communally in protected hibernacula such as abandoned animal burrows or rock crevices. **Where found:** mixed or short-grass prairie, badlands, sage flats, often near coulee or river bottoms; southwestern SK.

FISH

Fish are ectothermic vertebrates that live in the water, have streamlined bodies covered in scales, and possess fins and gills. A fundamental feature of fish is the serially repeated set of vertebrae and segmented muscles that allows the animal to move from side to side, propelling it through the water. A varying number of fins, depending on the species, further aid the fish to swim and navigate. Most fish are oviparous and lay eggs that are fertilized externally. Eggs are either produced in vast quantities and scattered or they are laid in a spawning nest (redd) under rocks or logs. Parental care may be present in the defence of such a nest or territory. Spawning can involve migrating long distances from inland rivers where reproduction occurs, back to open waters such as Lake Winnipeg or Hudson Bay.

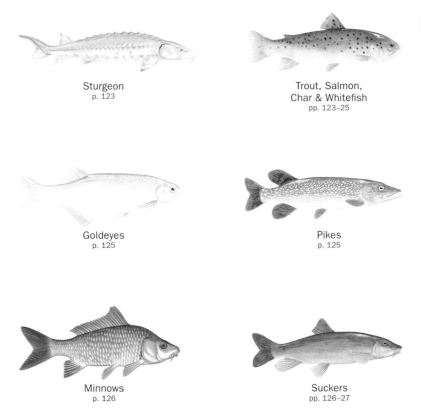

Sturgeon
p. 123

Trout, Salmon,
Char & Whitefish
pp. 123–25

Goldeyes
p. 125

Pikes
p. 125

Minnows
p. 126

Suckers
pp. 126–27

Catfish & Madtoms
p. 127

Burbot
p. 128

Sticklebacks
p. 128

Trout-perch
p. 128

Sunfishes & Bass
p. 129

Walleye, Perch & Drum
pp. 129–30

Sculpins
p. 130

Lake Sturgeon

Acipenser fulvescens

Length: 75 cm–1.45 m
(occasionally over 2 m)

For 100 million years, the lake sturgeon has nosed along river bottoms, using the 4 barbels that surround its mouth to detect prey. This scaleless relic has 5 rows of hard plates called "scutes" running down its body. • Unfortunately, this formerly abundant species is now threatened because of overharvesting of eggs for caviar, overfishing and habitat degradation. • Lake sturgeon can live up to 80 years, and individuals once grew to over 2 m in length, making it our largest freshwater fish. **Where found:** large lakes and rivers; central SK, much of MB.

Rainbow Trout

Oncorhynchus mykiss

Length: 30–46 cm
(maximum 91.5 cm)

Because of anglers' love of the rainbow trout, it has spread from western North America to 6 continents, becoming the most widely introduced species in the world. The trademark colourful appearance and heavily spotted back and sides vary in hue with lifestyle and habitat. • Rainbow trout in streams are bottom feeders but will often rise to the surface to leap for a struggling insect. They are highly respected by fly fishermen because of their spectacular jumps and fighting strength. **Where found:** cool, well-oxygenated waters; near swift currents in streams; southern two-thirds of SK/MB.

Brown Trout

Salmo trutta

Length: 25–40 cm
(maximum 87 cm)

The "brownie" was so much a part of European heritage that early settlers introduced "their" fish to North America and many other regions of the world. Many of the fish were either von Behr trout from Germany or Loch Leven trout from Scotland. Today, the populations are mixed and indistinguishable. • Brownies are drift feeders, preferring streams with cover and an intermediate water flow. They can handle warmer water temperatures and higher turbidity than other members of the trout family so may be introduced to streams disturbed by logging or industrial activity. **Where found:** various water bodies; sporadically in southern half of SK/MB.

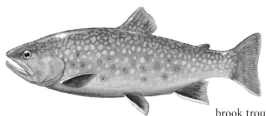

Brook Trout

Salvelinus fontinalis

Length: 15–25 cm
(maximum 86 cm)

The unique patterns of the brook trout make it hard to confuse with any other species. The vermiculations, or "worm tracks," on its back sets this handsome fish apart from our other fish. • The brook trout is actually a char, distinguishable from other char by the "jelly doughnuts" (red or yellow dots with blue halos) on its sides. Another fish with "jelly doughnuts," the brown trout, is a true trout and has a light body with black spots. • Native to eastern North America, brook trout were among the first fish introduced to other areas and have spread widely. **Where found:** cold, clear, slow-moving waters; clear shallow areas of lakes; sporadically throughout.

Lake Trout

Salvelinus namaycush

Length: 45–65 cm
(maximum 1 m)

Large, solitary lake trout prefer ice-cold water. In summer, they follow the retreat of colder water to the bottom of a lake, rarely making excursions into the warm surface layer. • Despite their slow growth, lake trout can reach old ages and large sizes. Large trout are often over 20 years old, with one granddaddy of a specimen reaching 62 years old! • Lake trout can take 6 years or more to reach maturity and may spawn only once every 2 to 3 years, making recovery from overfishing difficult. **Where found:** usually in deep, cooler lakes; throughout northern half of SK, much of MB, sporadically in south (e.g., Lake Diefenbaker). **Also known as:** laker.

Lake Whitefish

Coregonus clupeaformis

Length: 40 cm (maximum 63 cm)

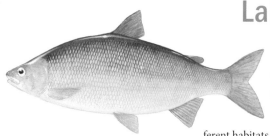

The lake whitefish is what biologists call a "plastic species": it changes behaviour, food habits and appearance in different habitats. One of the best identifiers for different forms is the number of gillrakers. Fish that live in more open water develop extended gillrakers that are better for filtering plankton. Lake whitefish caught closer to the surface tend to have higher gillraker counts than those that nibble food from the lake bottom. • This important commercial fish and the cisco *(C. artedii)* are the region's most common and widespread whitefish. **Where found:** cool, deep water at the bottom of larger lakes, occasionally in rivers; throughout.

Arctic Grayling

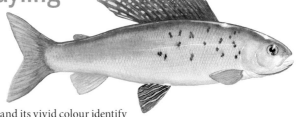

Thymallus arcticus

Length: 15–30 cm
(maximum 76 cm)

The arctic grayling's
large dorsal fin, the
aquatic equivalent of
deer or moose antlers, and its vivid colour identify
this species immediately. During spawning, this fish ventures from lakes and large
rivers to smaller tributaries, where each male aggressively defends its selected spawning ground. • A fish of cold, clear streams, the arctic grayling is vulnerable to
changes in the environment. This fish needs to see its food to catch it, so clean, clear
water is vital. **Where found:** clear, cold waters of large rivers, rocky creeks, lakes;
northern half of SK/MB.

Goldeye

Hiodon alosoides

Length: 35 cm
(maximum 50 cm)

In the early 1900s, a struggling
entrepreneur accidentally overheated
and smoked the goldeye he was trying to sell.
The flavour of "Winnipeg goldeye" won the taste buds of gourmets around the
world, and overfishing rapidly depleted stocks in Lake Winnipeg. • Goldeye eggs
are semi-bouyant, and they float safely undercover down the river for about 2 weeks
before hatching. Eggs released in Saskatchewan most likely hatch in Manitoba.
When an individual matures, it travels upstream, retracing the path the egg
originally took. • The closely related mooneye (*H. tergisus*) also occurs in our
southern waters. **Where found:** large, turbid waters; central and southern drainages.

Northern Pike

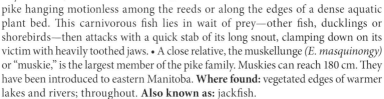

Esox lucius

Length: 46–76 cm
(maximum 1.3 m;
female is larger than male)

If you canoe, watch for adult
pike hanging motionless among the reeds or along the edges of a dense aquatic
plant bed. This carnivorous fish lies in wait of prey—other fish, ducklings or
shorebirds—then attacks with a quick stab of its long snout, clamping down on its
victim with heavily toothed jaws. • A close relative, the muskellunge *(E. masquinongy)*
or "muskie," is the largest member of the pike family. Muskies can reach 180 cm. They
have been introduced to eastern Manitoba. **Where found:** vegetated edges of warmer
lakes and rivers; throughout. **Also known as:** jackfish.

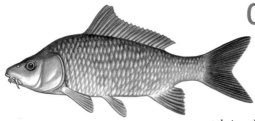

Common Carp

Cyprinus carpio

Length: 38–46 cm (maximum 1 m)

An omnivorous Eurasian fish introduced to North America in 1831, this abundant aquatic pest thrives throughout much of the continent's warmer water bodies. Carp, our largest minnow, forage along the bottom for food, uprooting and sucking in aquatic vegetation, then expelling it back into the water to separate edible items. These destructive feeding habits increase turbidity and destroy spawning, rearing and feeding grounds important for native fish and wildlife. Carp can greatly reduce or eliminate aquatic plant communities, thus affecting everything from dragonflies to nesting birds. **Where found:** eutrophic lakes, irrigation ditches, sewage outlets, ponds, rivers; warm, weedy, fairly shallow waters; throughout central and southern areas.

Emerald Shiner

Notropis atherinoides

Length: 5–7.5 cm (maximum 12 cm)

This baitfish is common in larger rivers and lakes and is important to many predators, both aquatic and avian. Populations fluctuate greatly, thus influencing the populations of many fish in the process. • These minnows spend much of their time in open water feeding on plankton, which they follow up to the surface at dusk. In autumn, large schools of these little jewels gather near shorelines and docks. • The related lake chub (*Couesius plumbeus*) is one of our most widespread and northerly minnows. It can survive in almost any pool or stream but prefers gravelly bottoms near rocky shores. **Where found:** open water of lakes, large rivers and shallow lakeshores in spring and autumn; throughout.

Longnose Sucker

Catostomus catostomus

Length: 30–50 cm (maximum 64 cm)

Scientists believe that suckers originated in Asia and then expanded their range to North America when the Bering land bridge linked the continents. With a lot of swimming, and the help of bait bucket releases, the longnose sucker is now found throughout Canada and southeast to Pennsylvania. • In spring, longnose suckers swim up smaller tributaries to spawn. Males develop a bright red lateral stripe. Watch for suckers where a stream riffles over a shallow rocky area or where a beaver dam creates a brushy waterfall. **Where found:** prefers cold lakes or rivers, occasionally in warmer, turbid waters; throughout central and northern regions.

White Sucker

Catostomus commersoni

Length: 25–41 cm (maximum 61 cm)

This abundant generalist species lives in habitats ranging from cold streams to warm, even polluted, waters. It avoids rapid currents and uses shallow areas to feed. • In early spring, hundreds of mating white suckers noisily splash and jostle in shallow streams or lakeshores. Animals such as other fish, eagles and bears depend on these spawning runs for food. Once hatched, the fry provide critical food for other young fish. **Where found:** variable habitats; prefers cool, clean waters with sandy or gravel substrate; throughout.

Black Bullhead

Ameiurus melas

Length: 7.5–25 cm (maximum 36 cm)

Black bullheads are probably best known for their habit of swallowing fishing hooks, and they seem to prefer being hooked over swimming free. • These catfish nose along, scavenging for almost anything edible, including aquatic insect larvae, crustaceans and small fish. Specialized sensory organs on their barbels allow bullheads to feed at night and in muddy waters. • The spines along the leading edge of the pectoral fins have poison glands that can sting unwary handlers. • Brown bullheads (*A. nebulosus*) are also found in similar habitats in our southern waters. **Where found:** turbid, slow moving waters; tolerant of pollutants and high water temperatures; southeastern SK, southern MB.

Channel Catfish

Ictalurus punctatus

Length: 37–53 cm (maximum 1.3 m)

The channel catfish is one of the largest and most sought-after members of the catfish family. • A slender fish with a long, wide head, 8 sensory barbels or "whiskers" around its mouth, and a deeply forked tail, its characteristics change considerably with size, sex, season and geographic location. • The specific epithet *punctatus* means "spotted" in Latin and refers to the dark spots scattered across this fish's body, though the spotting diminishes with age. **Where found:** cool, clear, deep waters, sometimes brackish water or lakes, larger rivers; southeastern SK and southern MB.

Burbot

Lota lota

Length: 30–80 cm
(maximum 1 m)

The burbot is the only member of the cod family confined to freshwater. • The single chin barbel and the pectoral fins contain taste buds. As these fish grow, they satisfy their ravenous appetite for whitefish and suckers by eating larger fish instead of increased numbers of smaller ones, sometimes swallowing fish almost as big as themselves. A 30-cm-long walleye was found in the stomach of a large burbot. • Once considered by anglers to be a "trash" fish, the burbot is gaining popularity among sport fishers. **Where found:** bottom of cold lakes and rivers; throughout.

Brook Stickleback

Culaea inconstans

Length: 5 cm
(maximum 8.7 cm)

This plentiful little fish is distinguished by 4 to 6 spines along its back. It is one of the easiest fish to see and can be found along the vegetated edges of water bodies. • Brook sticklebacks tolerate low oxygen levels and can live in waters where other fish cannot, even spreading into flooded fields that may eventually leave them high and dry. **Where found:** varied; ponds, saline sloughs, rivers, creeks, lake edges; aquatic vegetation is required for breeding; throughout except northern reaches.

Trout-perch

Percopsis omiscomaycus

Length: 7–10 cm
(maximum 13 cm)

Transparent skin make trout-perch fascinating: you can peer straight through to the body cavity if you look carefully, and you can actually see the 2 huge otoliths (ear bones) lying alongside the brain. • An important prey species for larger fish such as lake trout and burbot, trout-perch hide under rocks and usually feed at night. Shine a flashlight into the shallows on a dark June night and you may see the big eyes and chunky pale bodies of spawning trout-perch. They are one of the few non-salmonids with an adipose fin. **Where found:** usually deeper water but spawns and feeds in shallows; throughout.

Rock Bass

Ambloplites rupestris

Length: 12–17 cm

True to their name, these native game fish feed close to the rocks, near the current in streams and small rivers, using visual clues to locate crustaceans, smaller fish or other prey. • Also known as the "red eye," this fish's eye colour varies from orange to red. Like all bass, the 2 dorsal fins are connected; the first one is spiny and the second soft. The anal fin has 6 spines. • The black crappie (*P. nigromaculatus*) is another sunfish found in our southern drainages. **Where found:** near submerged trees, tangled roots, rocky ledges in medium-sized, southern rivers.

Smallmouth Bass

Micropterus dolomieui

Length: 20–30 cm
(maximum 68.6 cm)

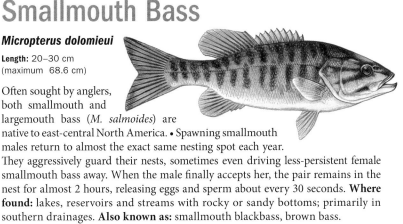

Often sought by anglers, both smallmouth and largemouth bass (*M. salmoides*) are native to east-central North America. • Spawning smallmouth males return to almost the exact same nesting spot each year. They aggressively guard their nests, sometimes even driving less-persistent female smallmouth bass away. When the male finally accepts her, the pair remains in the nest for almost 2 hours, releasing eggs and sperm about every 30 seconds. **Where found:** lakes, reservoirs and streams with rocky or sandy bottoms; primarily in southern drainages. **Also known as:** smallmouth blackbass, brown bass.

Yellow Perch

Perca flavescens

Length: 20–25 cm
(maximum 36 cm)

The yellow perch, with its recognizable black saddles, is often pictured in biology textbooks and dissected in science labs. It also falls prey to almost every piscivorous predator around, including other fish and birds. • Yellow perch lay eggs in gelatinous, accordion-folded ribbons that can be as long as a human is tall! These zigzag ribbons are draped over aquatic vegetation, an excellent strategy that keeps them away from suffocating bottom silt. Occasionally winds or waves cast segments, a unique find for lucky beachcombers. **Where found:** common in lakes, less common in rivers; throughout except northeastern MB.

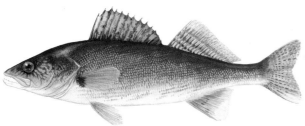

Walleye

Stizostedion vitreum

Length: 40–60 cm
(maximum 90 cm)

The walleye, prized
for its tasty flesh and
sporting qualities, has black and gold flecks all over its body and 2 dorsal fins. The
first dorsal fin is spiny, the second is fleshy. • The Red and Winnipeg rivers are
famous for their trophy-sized walleye, known as "greenbacks" because of their
iridescent green colour. • In "2-storey" lakes, brown trout inhabit the cool bottom
"storey," and walleye stick to the warmer surface waters and shallows. • The walleye is Saskatchewan's provincial fish emblem. **Where found:** large rivers, relatively deep lakes; prefers low amounts of light; throughout except extreme north.
Also known as: pickerel.

Iowa Darter

Etheostoma exile

Length: 4.5–6 cm
(maximum 7.5 cm)

Darters are the
warblers of the underwater
world—many species are unbelievably brightly coloured. In late winter, when
breeding season begins, the coloured pigments in male darters become much more
vibrant. At this time of year, male Iowa darters rival anything found in tropical
aquaria. • These tiny members of the perch family lack air bladders and thus don't
float. This adaptation allows them to better anchor on gravely stream bottoms,
where they seek small macro-invertebrate prey. **Where found:** among vegetation on
bottoms of lakes, reservoirs and slow-flowing rivers or creeks; SK, southern MB.

Slimy Sculpin

Cottus cognatus

Length: 7.5 cm
(maximum 13 cm)

The female slimy
sculpin literally falls "head over
tails" in love. After entering the burrow, she turns upside down to deposit her sticky
eggs on the underside of the rock or ledge that covers the den. More than one topsy-
turvy female may visit the nest, and the male guards his area for up to 5 weeks.
• Slimy sculpins are particularly fond of living under bridges, always a promising
place to look for local fish species. **Where found:** bottom dweller; usually in cool,
clean streams and lakes with rocky substrate; throughout.

INVERTEBRATES

Mountore than 95 percent of all animal species are invertebrates, and there are thousands of invertebrate species in our region. The few mentioned in this guide are frequently encountered and easily recognizable. Several aquatic species are included because exploring a pond with a bucket and dip net is a fun activity for children and a great way to introduce the concept of food chains. Invertebrates can be found in a variety of habitats and are an important part of most ecosystems. They provide food for birds, amphibians, shrews, bats and other insects, and they also play an important role in the pollination of plants and aid in the decay process.

Butterflies & Moths
pp. 132–34

Caterpillars
p. 135

Beetles
p. 136

Spruce Sawyer
p. 136

Crane Flies
p. 136

Ants, Bees & Wasps
p. 137

Sucking Bugs
p. 138

Lacewing
p. 138

Grasshopper
p. 138

Damselflies and Dragonflies
p. 139

Aquatic & Associates
pp. 140–41

Spiders
p. 142

Other Arthropods
p. 143

Cabbage White

Pieris rapae

Wingspan: 5 cm

Although a European introduction, this species is probably our most widely seen butterfly. The cabbage white was accidentally introduced near Montreal in the 1860s; since then, it has spread continent-wide. • The larvae feed on many types of mustards and can become localized pests. The green caterpillars are more than 3.5 cm long and are marked with 5 yellowish stripes; you probably encounter them on your cabbage plants. • This adaptable butterfly is easily the most urban of our species; it can appear anywhere, even in large cities. **Where found:** any open habitat; shuns large, dense forests; throughout.

Canadian Tiger Swallowtail

Papilio canadensis

Wingspan: about 10 cm

Few butterflies are more striking than these jumbo swallowtails. Tigers are fast, powerful fliers and often course high in the treetops. Fortunately, they often come down to our level for flower nectar. They turn up in gardens and are especially fond of dandelions. • The green caterpillars feed on various trees including aspen, willows and crabapple. They produce sticky silk and roll a leaf into a tent-like shelter during the day—a good bird-avoidance strategy. **Where found:** mature forests with appropriate host plants; adults range widely.

Spring Azure

Celastrina argiolus

Wingspan: 2.5 cm

As spring arrives in our region, the tiny spring azure can be seen fluttering along the forest floor before the last snows have melted. With brilliant blue upper wings, the male looks like a tiny flower come to life. The adult male patrols sheltered areas in search of his dull brown mate, which is found near red-osier dogwood or buffaloberry bushes. • Spring azures belong to a subfamily of butterflies commonly known as "blues." **Where found:** common in forest clearings; throughout.

Mourning Cloak

Nymphalis antiopa

Wingspan: 7 cm

These long-lived butterflies may survive for up to 10 months. Adults typically emerge in May or June to feed for a short time before taking shelter until autumn, when they become active again. As winter approaches, mourning cloaks shelter under a piece of bark or within a woodpile and hibernate until the spring mating season. You may be surprised to see a mourning cloak fluttering over the snow, but they will come out of hiding during warm spells, occasionally even in the middle of winter! **Where found:** widespread in forested areas; throughout.

Monarch

Danaus plexippus

Wingspan: about 9.5 cm

These familiar butterflies stage the most conspicuous and spectacular migration of any North American insect. In late summer and autumn, millions of monarchs begin moving southwestward toward Mexico. Ultimately, they over-winter in masses in high elevation fir forests. • Monarchs lay eggs on milkweed (*Asclepias* spp.), and their large caterpillars, banded with yellow, white and black, are often found on milkweed plants. When the caterpillars feed on milkweed, they absorb a toxic chemical into their bodies that makes both caterpillar and adult poisonous to birds. **Where found:** migrants can turn up in any open area that supports milkweed; southern and occasionally central areas.

Polyphemus Moth

Antherea polyphemus

Wingspan: 11 cm

This large moth is always noticed for its spectacular colours and design. Many people assume it's a butterfly, but moths have fuzzy or thin, pointy antennae and butterflies have slender antennae with thick tips. • The large eyespots exist for defensive purposes; if the wings are closed and a pred-ator, such as a bird, approaches, the polyphemus moth will flash its wings like eyelids, creating the illusion of a much larger creature to startle the predator. • Poly-phemus was a 1-eyed giant in Greek mythology—too bad this moth has 4 fake eyes and 2 real ones, for a total of 6. **Where found:** deciduous forests; throughout.

Woolly Bear Caterpillar

Lophocampa maculata

Length: 4–5 cm

These fuzzy, black and yellow beasts are the offspring of the spotted tussock moth and are a common sight in late summer. They can be seen crawling through yards, gardens or along trails when they climb down from their host plants and wander along the ground in search of a pupation site. They often spin their cocoons under railway ties, rain barrels or logs. Larvae host plants include Manitoba maple, alder, willow, cherry and linden. • According to folklore, the amount of black on this caterpillar indicated how severe the upcoming winter would be (more black meant more severe). **Where found:** meadows, pastures, roadsides; throughout except northern areas.

Tent Caterpillar

Malacosoma **spp.**

Length: 4–5 cm

Every decade or so, regional outbreaks of tent caterpillars occur, but populations may soar in one area while remaining stable in another. The tent caterpillars in our region have similar life cycles. The short-lived, yellowish brown moths emerge in July, around the same time that female tent caterpillars lay up to 300 eggs on a host plant. The female moths then cover the eggs with a frothy substance that hardens to a dark, protective coating. Eggs hatch in spring when the host plant leafs out. The caterpillars begin to munch on the leaves, and most species spin their characteristic silken tents, which serve as resting places, in the crotches of trees. **Where found:** forested areas; throughout.

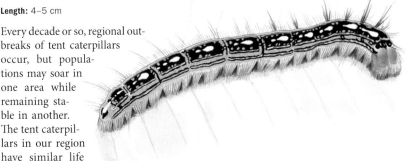

135

Multicoloured Asian Ladybug

Harmonia axyridis

Length: 5 mm

These charming Asian invaders were released by the U.S. Department of Agriculture during the 1920s as a biological control for crop-damaging aphids. They finally took, and now many households are plagued with swarms of the cute little pests as they enter houses to hibernate. Evidence suggests these invasive little beetles have out-competed native species in some areas, and they are now the most common species of ladybug in some places. • These ladybugs usually have a 10-spot pattern on an orange back, but black and unmarked forms also occur. **Where found:** nearly anywhere, often enters buildings; throughout.

Spruce Sawyer

Monochamus scutellatus

Length: 20 mm, plus long antennae

Finding this miniature replica of the Asian longhorn beetle in your backyard is a thrill. The exotic-looking spruce sawyer has a white-flecked ebony body and long, curved antennae. This marvellous beast pupates inside a dead spruce tree, and the larva hollows out winding galleries through the wood. When the awkward, noisy adult emerges to mate, it flies with its body held vertically and its legs sticking out in all directions. **Where found:** within the forested areas of our region where there are spruce trees.

Crane Fly

Holorusia spp.

Length: up to 3.5 cm

These innocent insects are not giant mosquitoes or garden harvestmen ("daddy longlegs") but very benign and harmless crane flies. Giant crane flies do not bite, and their larvae only scavenge in soil and rotting logs. • The crane is an appropriate analogy to these long-legged creatures, which are more comfortable in the forest than when they accidentally find themselves inside your house. **Where found:** forested areas.

Carpenter Ant

Camponotus pennsylvanicus

Length: 10–15 mm

Woe to homeowners with a colony of these wood-borers in their houses. Carpenter ants damage the wooden infra-structure of a home. Their presence is characterized by small tunnels, or galleries, with occasional slit-like openings where they expel sawdust. The ants don't actually eat the wood, as do termites; they are making nests. Carpenter ants do best in wood with a moisture content of 15% or higher. • In the wild, they excavate trees and form extensive galleries. Pileated woodpeckers readily tune into these colonies and often rip apart large sections of bark to get at the ants. **Where found:** forested areas of SK/MB.

Bumblebee

Bombus spp.

Length: 14–20 mm

These large, fuzzy bees are intimidating but not aggressive, and they can be closely approached. • Their dense, hairy coats help warm them, and "bumbles" can often fly in cooler weather than many other insects. Their hairy coats also make them extremely effective pollinators; as they visit flowers, the pollen adheres readily to their "fur" and is transferred to other plants. • Bumblebees usually build nests in underground burrows, and only young queens survive the winter to start new colonies the next spring. **Where found:** open habitats, frequent visitors to flowers and gardens; throughout.

Yellow Jacket

Vespula spp.

Length: 10–15 mm

Big and boldly striped in black and yellow, these ill-tempered hornets are attracted to sweets, including pop. • The yellow jacket nests in trees or in old rodent ground burrows and lives in a papery nest made of wood fibre chewed into a pulp. People mowing lawns or walking through the woods can sometimes agitate a colony and be attacked. A yellowjacket's painful sting can be inflicted over and over again, unlike a honeybee's. • These predators kill a variety of other insects and sometimes eat nectar at flowers such as goldenrod. **Where found:** nearly ubiquitous in open areas; throughout.

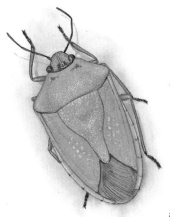

Green Stink Bug

Chlorochroa sayi

Length: 14–19 mm

There is no question about it: stink bugs stink. They are easily recognizable by their unique odour, (produced by their scent glands), their shield-shaped body and the triangular plate (scutellum) in the centre of their back. • The female stink bug lays clusters of intricately shaped eggs on the surface of a leaf. The mother guards the eggs until they hatch, then leaves the brood to fend for itself. **Where found:** woodlands and agricultural fields; southern half of region.

Green Lacewing

Chrysopa spp.

Length: about 10 mm

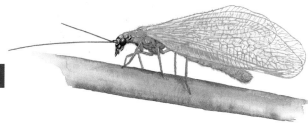

Lacewings are frequent visitors to your garden, where their lime green bodies blend into the light foliage of young plants. They have elegant filigreed wings (hence lacewing), large golden eyes and, if you pick one up, you will notice they produce an odd scent. • Both the adults and the larvae of these beneficial insects feed on aphids. **Where found:** shrubby or forested areas, gardens; throughout.

Road Duster Grasshopper

Dissosteira carolina

Length: 13–14 cm

One of North America's largest and most conspicuous grasshoppers, this big bug is easy enough to miss when motionless, but wait until it flushes. In flight, the road duster flashes large, black wings rimmed with pale gold, suggesting a mourning cloak butterfly. In flight, its wings make loud crackling sounds called crepitations. • Males engage in a courtship display in which they hover like tiny helicopters low over the ground. • Road dusters can become so abundant locally that they can damage plants. **Where found:** nearly any open ground, often weedy roadsides and lots; southern two-thirds of SK/MB.

Boreal Bluet

Enallagma boreale

Length: 3 cm

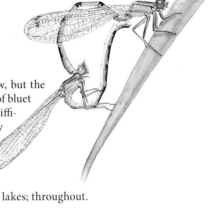

Nearly every pond or lake will host
this familiar blue damselfly. The
female may sometimes be green or yellow, but the
male is always blue. Several other species of bluet
are also found in our area and are quite difficult to tell apart. To distinguish a damselfly
from a dragonfly, however, notice that
damselflies are thin, and all 4 of their
wings are similar in shape and are
(usually) folded up over their backs.
Where found: among reeds in ponds and lakes; throughout.

Green Darner

Anax junius

Length: up to 8 cm

Like monarch butterflies, green darners are
highly migratory, but their movements are not as
well understood. Sometimes massive swarms, number-
ing into the thousands, are seen moving in autumn on
a steady southwestern trajectory that probably ends in
the southern states or Mexico. • Green darners, like
all dragonflies, are voracious hunters. Each time they
zig and zag in the air, they seize small insect prey. Darners have incredible vision:
each compound eye is composed of thousands of tiny facets—each, in effect, a tiny
eyelet. **Where found:** any open water, migrants can be seen anywhere; throughout.

Cherry-faced Meadowhawk

Sympetrum internum

Length: 35 mm

The little red or yellow dragonflies
that can be so common in parks
and gardens are the meadowhawks.
The cherry-faced meadowhawk is one of the
most common species. The male has a cherry
red face and a deep red body; the female and young male are yellowish.
• Dragonflies breed in ponds, but meadowhawks will wander far from water to feed.
You can sneak up and get a good look at them because they often perch on or close
to the ground. **Where found:** marshy ponds and lakes, streamsides; throughout.

Mayfly

Hexagenia spp.

Length: 5–30 mm

Mayflies spend the majority of their lives near water, developing for several years as aquatic larvae then moulting twice within a matter of hours to emerge as adults. The short-lived adults have no feeding mouthparts and survive on land for only one day, swarming together to mate. Males die soon after mating, but the females drop back down to the water, where they lay their eggs before perishing. Anglers celebrate these spectacular hatches that attract feeding trout to the surface. • Amazingly, mayfly hatches have been linked to the bloom time of specific flowering plants, which vary annually with changes in temperature and light. The seasonal rhythm of lifecycle events, in this case the connection between insects, flowers and fish, falls under a branch of science known as phenology. **Where found:** near water; throughout.

Virile Crayfish

Orconectes virilis

Length: 10–12 cm

Crayfish are fearsome-looking crustaceans with large, lobster-like pincers. Mostly nocturnal, they spend the day sheltering under rocks or logs, hiding from predators. They also tunnel into soft, muddy ground. Long, sensitive antennae help them feel their way as they range overland, especially on rainy nights. • Virile crayfish are native from Alberta to Québec and into the northern U.S. but have been introduced farther south by anglers who use them as bait. Introduction of non-native crayfish has led to localized declines in some native crayfish. **Where found:** ponds, lakes, streams, wetlands; central and southern SK/MB.

Water Strider

Gerris buenoi

Length: 13 mm

This unique bug lives on the surface of the water, relying on surface tension and 4 long, water-repellent legs to keep afloat. The water strider's legs distribute its body weight over the water's surface and allow the bug to zing about at up to 1.5 m per second, leaving rings of water in its wake. • This sucking bug uses its 2 short, front legs to catch larvae or other insects that fall into the water. In turn, fish and birds eat the water strider. **Where found:** ponds, lakes, slow-moving streams; throughout. **Also known as:** pond skater.

Caddisfly Larvae

Order Trichoptera

Length: with case, up to 60 mm

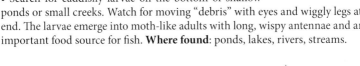

Here are larvae worth looking for! These tiny architects build a protective casing or shell around their soft bodies by gluing together sand, twigs or leaves using saliva and silk. The tube-shaped or coiled casings act as camouflage.
• Search for caddisfly larvae on the bottom of shallow ponds or small creeks. Watch for moving "debris" with eyes and wiggly legs at one end. The larvae emerge into moth-like adults with long, wispy antennae and are an important food source for fish. **Where found**: ponds, lakes, rivers, streams.

Water Boatman

Family Corixidae

Length: 8 mm

This skilled diver carries a bubble of air under its abdomen to use much like a primitive scuba tank. If you keep a water boatman in a clear jar, you can see how it breathes from the bubble. • This creature's 3 sets of legs are each adapted for a specific function: digging in mud for food, holding on to plants and rocks underwater or swimming and maneuvring. **Where found:** ponds, lakes, rivers, streams; throughout.

Giant Diving Beetles

Order Coleoptera

Length: 1–4 cm

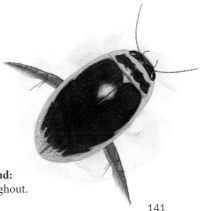

Equipped with a hard exoskeleton, large, efficient swimming limbs, and sharp, chewing mouthparts, diving beetles are ferocious and impressive aquatic hunters. To breathe underwater, they dive with a bubble of air taken from the surface. • These beetles breed and lay their eggs on land, where the young pupate in damp forest soils before flying to water as adults. • There are many species of diving beetles in our region. **Where found:** marshes, ponds, slow-moving streams; throughout.

Fishing Spider

Dolomedes triton

Length: *Male:* half the size of female;
Female: over 7.5 cm, including outstretched legs

These terrifying-looking spiders occasionally wander into homes, causing horror and excitement. Although they are menacing in appearance, fishing spiders rarely bite people and, like most spiders, are safe enough if not harassed. They are normally found near water and can even run over the water's surface in pursuit of prey. • Fishing spiders usually feed on small insects, but they can capture small fish. **Where found:** quiet waters of streams, ponds, wetlands but will range considerable distances from water; throughout.

Orbweavers

Araneus spp.

Length: 9–20 mm (body only)

Spiders that make the classic "orb" webs belong to the orb-weaver group, like the famous spider in *Charlotte's Web*. Their familiar, flat webs have radiating spokes connected by spiral silk strands. When prey hits the web, these spiders rush forth and quickly enwrap it in silk from their spinnerets. After completely immobilizing the victim, they administer the *coup de grâce*: several venom-filled bites from sharp fangs. There are about 2 dozen species in our region. **Where found:** various habitats; throughout.

Harvestmen

Order Opiliones

Length: about 5 mm (body only); legs span 15 cm

Numerous species are in this poorly studied group of spider relatives called "daddy longlegs," but most are readily recognizable as harvestmen. They climb about in shrubs or on the forest floor hunting small insects and occasionally feeding on plant sap. Unlike true spiders, harvestmen cannot produce silk and do not have venom glands or fangs, so they are utterly harmless. • Fossils from the Order Opilones date back 400 million years. Today, the order may contain over 10,000 species worldwide, but much work remains to sort them out. **Where found:** nearly all habitats; throughout.

Garden Centipedes

Lithobius spp.

Length: up to 3 cm

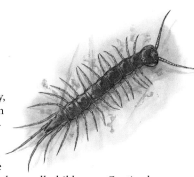

A centipede moves its many legs very quickly, but if you manage to see one sitting still, you can count 1 set of legs per body segment—significantly less than 100 feet, as the name suggests. • This predator has venomous fangs with which it subdues its prey. It is not dangerous to people but nevertheless should be avoided, especially by small children. • Centipedes require a moist environment to survive and will quickly desiccate if they find their way into a house. **Where found:** under moist debris or cover in gardens and forests.

Sowbug

Oniscus asellus

Length: about 1 cm

Sowbugs are slow-moving, heavily armoured creatures with a segmented shell and many legs. Native to Europe, they began showing up in our region in the 1970s and have been becoming more common ever since. These crustaceans are found in damp places, including city gardens and occasionally basements. Sowbugs are not harmful and feed on decaying plants and animals. **Where found:** damp places, mainly in cities; status unknown but spreading.

Northern Scorpion

Paruroctonus boreus

Length: 3.5 cm

The dry grasslands region in the southwest corner of Saskatchewan is the only area in Canada warm enough for the northern scorpion. It spends most of the day hiding under rocks and hunts for small bugs at night. You may find it by using a flashlight, or try putting a "black light" bulb in a camping light—scorpions glow green under ultraviolet light. Some scorpions can be deadly venomous, but to humans, the northern scorpion's sting is no worse than a bee sting. Remember to treat these rare animals with respect and let them go about their business. **Where found:** arid grasslands; only in southwestern corner of SK.

PLANTS

Plants belong to the Kingdom Plantae. They are autotrophic, which means they produce their own food from inorganic materials through a process called photosynthesis. Plants are the basis of all food webs. They supply oxygen to the atmosphere, modify climate and create and hold soil in place. They disperse their seeds and pollen through carriers such as wind, water and animals. Fossil fuels come from ancient deposits of organic matter—largely that of plants. In this book, plants are separated into 3 categories: trees and tall shrubs; shrubs and vines; and forbs, ferns and grasses.

TREES & TALL SHRUBS

Trees are long-lived, woody plants that are normally taller than 5 metres. This section also includes some tall shrubs. There are 2 types of trees: conifers and broadleaf. Conifers, or cone-bearers, have needles or small, scale-like leaves. Most conifers are evergreens, but some shed their leaves in winter. Most broadleaf trees lose their leaves in autumn and are often called deciduous trees (meaning "falling off" in Latin).

Trees provide a windbreak, camouflage, shelter or a food source for many animals. Roots host a multitude of beneficial fungi, support certain parasitic plants and bind soil, preventing erosion. Trunks provide a substrate for moss and lichen, which many animals use for shelter and nesting material. Tree cavities are used by everything from owls to squirrels to snakes. Leafy canopies support an amazing diversity of life, including arboreal species we don't fully understand. A diversity of wildlife feed on seed cones and fruit.

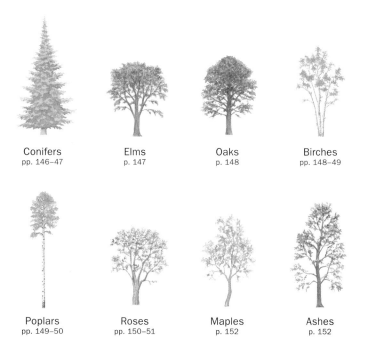

Conifers
pp. 146–47

Elms
p. 147

Oaks
p. 148

Birches
pp. 148–49

Poplars
pp. 149–50

Roses
pp. 150–51

Maples
p. 152

Ashes
p. 152

Balsam Fir

Abies balsamea

Height: up to 25 m
Needles: 15–25 mm long; flat, flexible
Seed cones: 4–10 cm long; erect, greyish brown

Balsam fir needles have 2 white lines on the lower surface. Erect, barrel-shaped cones usually grow near the top of the tree's spire-like crown. • Cut trees do not immediately shed their needles, making this species a popular Christmas tree. The wood is used as pulp, and the resin, sold as "Canada balsam," is used as a mounting material for microscope slides, as glue and in candle- and soap-making. The oil-rich seeds are eaten by many species of birds, porcupines and squirrels. Spruce grouse forage on the leaves. **Where found:** low, swampy ground to well-drained hillsides; requires moist soil; central SK/MB.

White Spruce

Picea glauca

Height: 25–40 m
Needles: 15–20 mm long; stiff, 4-sided
Seed cones: 15–60 mm long; cylindrical, pale brown

Small white spruce often grow beneath old jack pines. This species can live for 200 years and eventually replaces pines in mature forests. It is a good choice for landscaping and is used in reforestation. • Spruce needles roll between your fingers, unlike the flat, 2-sided needles of fir. • Traditionally, Native peoples used the flexible roots to lace together birch-bark canoes. • This tree is an important source of food and shelter for many forest animals, including grouse and seed-eating birds, porcupines and red squirrels. • White spruce is Manitoba's provincial tree. **Where found:** various soils and climates, but prefers moist, rich soil; throughout except southern grasslands.

Black Spruce

Picea mariana

Height: up to 15 m (rarely to 30 m)
Needles: 8–15 mm long; stiff, 4-sided
Seed cones: 2–3 cm long; dull greyish brown to purplish brown

This slow-growing wetland tree, which may live for 200 years, is an important source of lumber and pulp. • Northern explorers used black spruce to make spruce beer, a popular drink that prevented scurvy. Spruce gum was also chewed or boiled into cough syrup to relieve sore throats (spruce should be used in moderation). • Snowshoe hares love to eat young spruce seedlings and red squirrels harvest the cones, but in general black spruce is not favoured as a wildlife food source. • Many black spruce have a club-shaped crown. **Where found:** well-drained, moist flatlands in north to cool, damp, boggy sites in south; throughout except southern grasslands.

Tamarack

Larix laricina

Height: up to 20 m (rarely to 25 m)
Needles: 2–5 cm long; soft, deciduous
Seed cones: 1–2 cm long; 20 or fewer scales, pale brown

The leaves of this slender, exotic-looking tree are unusual among conifers: they turn golden yellow and drop in autumn. They grow on stubby twigs in tightly spiraled tufts of 15–60. • Straight tamarack trunks are used as poles, piers and railway ties. The tannin-rich bark was used for tanning leather. • European larch *(L. decidua)* is often used in landscaping. It has larger cones (up to 4 cm long) with 40–60 scales and bright green needles in tufts of 30–55. **Where found:** moist, well-drained soils, bogs, muskeg; throughout except southern grasslands.

Jack Pine

Pinus banksiana

Height: up to 20 m (maximum 27 m)
Needles: 2–4 cm long; straight, slightly twisted
Seed cones: 25–75 mm long; yellowish brown, closed, straight or curved inward

Jack pines are the first conifers to colonize areas burned by fire. The cones are held shut with a tight resin bond that melts when heated, allowing the seeds to disperse. • Cones usually occur in groups of 2 to 3 and point toward the tip of the branch. The needles grow in bundles of 2. • Animals and birds browse on young jack pine seedlings and eat the fallen seeds. **Where found:** dry, infertile, acidic, often sandy or rocky soils; throughout except southern grasslands.

White Elm

Ulmus americana

Height: up to 30 m
Leaves: 10–15 cm long; asymmetrical bases
Flowers: small; in tassel-like clusters
Fruit: winged nutlets, 8–10 mm long

Large, graceful elm trees once lined our city streets and parks, but hundreds of thousands have been lost to Dutch elm disease since its arrival in Canada in the 1940s. This species is still abundant in the wild but seldom gets very large before being attacked and killed by the fungal infection. Occasional giants still occur as isolated specimens in the midst of agricultural fields, where the disease cannot readily reach them. • White elms are very important as hosts for many species of butterflies and moths. Some of the butterflies that commonly use elms are the question mark *(Polygonia interrogationis),* the comma *(Polygonia* spp.) and the mourning cloak *(Nymphalis antiopa).* **Where found:** generally bottomlands, stream terraces, sheltered slopes; southern SK/MB.

Bur Oak

Quercus macrocarpa

Height: up to 15 m
Leaves: 10–30 cm long; rounded lobes
Flowers: male in hanging catkins
Fruit: acorns 2–3 cm long, large cup encloses half or more of nut

There are 2 major groups of oaks. Leaves in the white oak group (which includes bur oak) have rounded lobes that lack bristle tips. Red oaks typically have sharper-angled lobes terminated by bristles. • The nutritious acorns can be eaten raw but were traditionally ground or roasted and used as a flour substitute, soup thickener or caffeine-free coffee substitute. Many animals consume the acorns. • Bur oaks are often grown in city parks and gardens as shade trees or ornamentals. Their deep roots and thick bark make them fire and drought resistant. **Where found:** deep, rich bottomlands to rocky uplands, mixed with other trees; southeastern SK, central and southern MB.

Paper Birch

Betula papyrifera

Height: up to 25 m
Leaves: 5–10 cm long; coarsely toothed
Flowers: tiny; hanging pollen catkins 7–9 cm long; erect seed catkins 8 mm long
Fruit: tiny; flat, 2-winged nutlets in hanging seed catkins

This showy, small tree occurs across North America. It has peeling, creamy white bark and leaves with 5–9 straight veins per side. Native peoples used the tree for birch-bark canoes, baskets and message paper. To shield against snow blindness, they made "sunglasses" using bark strips with lenticels. • This pioneer species thrives in full sun and nutrient-rich habitats. In burned or cut areas, it can form near monocultures. • Birch bark is a winter staple for moose and white-tailed deer. Porcupines and snowshoe hares browse on the leaves, seedlings and bark, and common redpolls eat the catkins. **Where found:** open, often disturbed sites, forest edges on a variety of substrates; throughout except tundra.

Water Birch

Betula occidentalis

Height: up to 12 m
Leaves: 2–5 cm long; broadly oval, sharply toothed
Flowers: 2–6 cm long; catkins
Fruit: slender catkins and hairy, winged nutlets, 2.5–4 cm long

When mature, water birch has dark purplish brown bark that does not peel off like that of paper birch. Its leaves have 4–5 veins per side. This tall shrub grows in moist, riparian areas and is often found in pure, dense stands or mixed with streamside shrubs such as willows or alders. • Liquid, slightly sweet birch sap can be collected in spring and used as a beverage or boiled into syrup. **Where found:** moist areas, streamsides; throughout except eastern MB and tundra.

Speckled Alder

Alnus incana ssp. *rugosa*

Height: up to 8 m
Leaves: 5–10 cm long; deep veined, double-toothed
Flowers: 5–8 cm long; mature pollen catkins
Fruit: mature catkins oval, cone-like, 10–15 mm long

These tall, clumped deciduous shrubs often grow near lakes and rivers but do not tolerate shade. The woody, cone-like fruits are made of tiny, broadly winged nutlets. The leaves are shiny green and finely toothed. • The wood was an important fuel for smoking fish, meat and hides. The twigs and inner bark produce a red-brown dye that was used to colour hides and birch-bark baskets. • Green alder (*A. virdis*) is shade-tolerant and grows as an understorey plant on both wet sites and dry, upland sites. **Where found:** streamsides, moist sites; throughout except tundra.

Trembling Aspen

Populus tremuloides

Height: 10–20 m
Leaves: 2–8 cm; finely toothed
Flowers: tiny; in slender, hanging catkins 2–10 cm long
Fruit: numerous hairless capsules, in hanging, downy catkins 10 cm long

Suckers from the shallow, spreading roots of this deciduous tree can colonize many hectares of land. Single trunks are short lived, but a colony (clone) can survive for thousands of years. Aspen are gorgeous in autumn, when bright yellow foliage contrasts with silvery bark. • The greenish, photosynthetic bark produces a white powder to protect the trees from ultraviolet radiation in open areas. This powder can be used as sunscreen. These trees are sometimes called "asbestos trees" because the trunk will not burn easily when a fast-moving fire passes through the forest. **Where found:** dry to moist sites; throughout except southern SK grasslands. **Also known as:** quaking aspen, aspen poplar.

Eastern Cottonwood

Populus deltoides

Height: up to 30 m
Leaves: 5–10 cm long; rounded triangular shape
Flowers: 5–7 cm long; catkins
Fruit: capsules, 8–12 mm long, in 15–25 cm long, hanging, downy catkins

Cottonwoods grow on floodplains or shorelines because the seeds require wet mud to germinate. The trees begin to "snow" in late May or early June, as rivers swollen from spring runoff begin to recede. These fast-growing trees can reach massive proportions—old cottonwoods are among the largest trees in many areas. Young trees can grow more than 3.5 m a year, and even big ones can add 1.5 m annually. **Where found:** moist, warm, low-lying sites, floodplains, sand dunes near lakes; central and southern SK, southern MB.

Balsam Poplar

Populus balsamifera

Height: up to 25 m
Leaves: 5–12 cm long; broadly ovate, long-stalked
Flowers: 7–10 cm long; catkins
Fruit: catkins, 10–13 cm, with small, oval seed capsules

The trunks of these trees can reach girths of up to 1 m, with bark becoming deeply furrowed and dark grey when old. This tree had several traditional uses in native medicines, as well as being a source of sugar, fragrance, ink and tipi firewood. • The male and female flowers are in catkins on separate trees, and the seeds are in capsules attached to parachutes of cottony down. Young seedlings have extremely large leaves to ensure maximum energy absorption. • Ungulates browse on the young trees, and bees collect the sticky, aromatic resin from the buds to cement and waterproof their hives. **Where found:** moist, low-lying areas; throughout to tundra.

Pin Cherry

Prunus pensylvanica

Height: up to 12 m
Leaves: 3–10 cm long; slender, sharp-pointed
Fruit: 6–8 mm; red drupes
Flowers: white, 5-petals, 1 cm across, in clusters

Pin cherries have a lifespan of about 40 years, and mature trees produce edible, sour fruit. Tart wild cherries can be cooked, strained and sweetened for use in jellies, jams or syrup. **Caution:** The stones, bark, wood and leaves of cherry trees contain hydrocyanic acid and are toxic, so only the cherry flesh can be used. • Pin cherries can also be planted as ornamentals, and the flowering plants attract an audible number of bees in spring. Songbirds feast on the berries and disperse the seeds, giving rise to the name "bird cherry." **Where found:** open woodlands or recently burned sites; throughout SK/MB except tundra.

Chokecherry

Prunus virginiana

Height: up to 8 m
Leaves: 3–10 cm long; broadly oval with sharp tip
Flowers: tiny; white cup flowers hang in clusters
Fruit: reddish to blackish drupes, 8–12 mm across

Chokecherry has long, bottlebrush-like clusters of flowers and hanging clusters of shiny, crimson fruit that turn black with age. The sour fruit of mature trees can be eaten raw or used in jellies, jams or wine. Dried chokecherries were an important trade item for indigenous peoples in Canada. **Caution:** the stones, bark, wood and leaves contain hydrocyanic acid and are toxic, so only the cherry flesh can be used. • Many species of moths and butterflies, including the tiger swallowtail, use chokecherry as a host plant. **Where found:** open sites, fencerows, streams, forest edges; southern two-thirds of SK/MB.

Showy Mountain-ash

Sorbus decora

Height: up to 15 m
Leaves: 3–8 cm long; pinnately divided into 13–17 opposite leaflets
Flowers: tiny; white, in dense 5–10 cm wide clusters
Fruit: shiny, red-orange berry-like pomes, 8–10 mm across

This extremely showy tree has bluish green leaves and bright clusters of white flowers or glossy clusters of reddish berries. The juicy berrie attract many birds such as waxwings. • Western mountain-ash (*S. sitchensis*) is widespread through the boreal forest of northern Saskatchewan. **Where found:** riparian areas, moist lower slopes; scattered and local in central and southern MB.

Hawthorn spp.

Crataegus **spp.**

Height: up to 10 m
Leaves: 2–10 cm long; leathery, ovate, wedge-shaped base
Flowers: 1–2 cm across, white, in loose, flat-topped clusters
Fruit: red haws (pomes), 8–10 mm

Numerous hawthorn species grow throughout southern Canada, and distinguishing among them can drive even accomplished botanists mad. Most of this easily recognized species are quite thorny and have branched clusters of white, unpleasant-smelling flowers and reddish haws that remain on the plant throughout winter. Look for thorny branches and larger leaves growing off the flowering shoots. • Hawthorn thickets provide shelter and food for many small animals that, in turn, help distribute the fruit. **Where found:** open, disturbed sites such as old pastures; southern SK/MB.

Saskatoon

Amelanchier alnifolia

Height: up to 4 m
Leaves: 2–5 cm long; oval to round
Flowers: about 1 cm across; white, showy, 5-petals, in clusters
Fruit: dark purple berry-like pomes, 5–10 mm wide

These hardy, deciduous shrubs or small trees have beautiful white blossoms in spring, delicious fruit in summer and scarlet leaves in autumn. • The sweet, juicy "berries" of this shrub were an important food source for many Native peoples. Large quantities were dried and mixed with meat and fat, or added to stews. Today, saskatoons are used in baked goods, jams, jellies, syrups and wine. Many mammals and birds also feast on the berries, including black bears, snowshoe hares, flying squirrels, pheasants, grouse, woodpeckers and songbirds. **Where found:** dry, often sandy woods, rocky sites, forest edges; throughout to tundra.

Mountain Maple

Acer spicatum

Height: 3–5 m
Leaves: 5–12 cm long; broad, 3–5 lobed, coarse toothed
Flowers: 1 cm across; pale yellowish green, in dense erect clusters
Fruit: samaras, 2 cm long

This small maple tree is our most northerly ranging maple species, found well into the boreal forest. It is identified in summer by opposite leaves with 3 prominent lobes (sometimes 2 lower lobes) and small scarlet to pinkish brown keys (samaras), spreading at a 90° angle or less. The yellowish green flower clusters stand erect. • Mountain maple has no commercial value, but the branches spread toward the ground, take root and grow into dense thickets, controlling erosion on steep banks and ravines. **Where found:** moist, mixed woods, thickets; east-central SK, central MB.

Manitoba Maple

Acer negundo

Height: up to 20 m
Leaves: 5–12 cm long; opposite, irregularly coarse-toothed, divided into 3–5 leaflets
Flowers: tiny; pale yellowish green, male in hairy bundles, female in clusters
Fruit: pair of winged samaras, 3–5 cm long, hanging in clusters

This species might not be recognized as a maple at first glance because of its trifoliate leaves, which suggest poison ivy. Manitoba maple is our only maple with compound leaves. • This widely planted, fast-growing shade or shelterbelt tree can withstand drought and freezing temperatures, but snow, ice and wind can cause its weak branches to break. • Samaras usually spread at less than a 45° angle, and the hanging clusters of fruit persist through winter. The abundant samaras provide many seed-eating birds, including evening grosbeaks, as well as rodents and squirrels with an important winter food source. **Where found:** low, moist sites, disturbed ground, especially along streams; central and southern SK/MB. **Also known as:** box-elder.

Green Ash

Fraxinus pennsylvanica

Height: up to 25 m
Leaves: 10–15 cm long; opposite, pinnately divided into 5–9 (usually 7) leaflets
Flowers: tiny; purplish to yellow, in compact clusters along twigs
Fruit: slender, winged samaras 28–60 mm long

Green ash is a widely distributed species in Canada and grows in wet, poorly drained sites. The long, tapered leaves have short stalks and are shallow-toothed above the middle. Green ash samaras are very slender and elongate, and the actual seed below the wing is needle-like, compared to the much plumper and cylindrical seeds of other ashes. • Green ash is used for canoe paddles and other sporting goods, as well as tool handles and picture frames. The bark produces a red dye. **Where found:** moist to wet sites, floodplains, swamps; central and southern SK/MB. **Also known as:** red ash.

SHRUBS & VINES

The difference between a tree and a shrub is sometimes rather sketchy, but in general, shrubs are small woody plants less than 5 metres tall. They are typically bushy owing to multiple small trunks and branches that emerge from near the ground, and many species produce soft berries. Some shrubs occur in open, sunny areas, and others are important dominant components of the understorey in forests. They provide habitat and shelter for a variety of animals, and their berries, leaves and often bark are crucial sources of food. The tasty berries of some shrubs have been a staple of Native and traditional foods, and they are still enjoyed by people throughout our region.

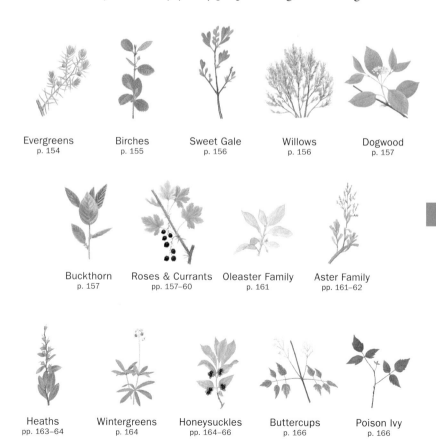

Evergreens
p. 154

Birches
p. 155

Sweet Gale
p. 156

Willows
p. 156

Dogwood
p. 157

Buckthorn
p. 157

Roses & Currants
pp. 157–60

Oleaster Family
p. 161

Aster Family
pp. 161–62

Heaths
pp. 163–64

Wintergreens
p. 164

Honeysuckles
pp. 164–66

Buttercups
p. 166

Poison Ivy
p. 166

Common Juniper

Juniperus communis

Height: up to 1 m
Needles: 5–12 mm long; narrow, lance-shaped
Seed cones: female 6–10 mm across, bluish, berry-like; male catkin-like cones

Common juniper grows over much of the world and is most famous as the flavouring for gin. The blue-grey "berries" of this shrub are, in fact, tiny cones with 3–8 fleshy scales. The strongly flavoured berries are occasionally added to wild game dishes but are generally considered distasteful. Pregnant women or people with kidney problems should not eat juniper. • Creeping juniper (*J. horizontalis*), also widespread in our region, is a low, creeping evergreen shrub (up to 25 cm tall) with overlapping, scale-like leaves. **Where found:** dry, open sites; throughout.

Crowberry

Empetrum nigrum

Height: creeping evergreen, to 15 cm
Leaves: 3–8 mm; needle-like
Flowers: tiny; purplish crimson
Fruit: berry-like drupes, 4–8 mm

This creeping, evergreen shrub forms dense mats on the forest floor. It is commonly found in cool, spruce forests, muskeg and on tundra. • The black, edible berries may be harvested in autumn or the following spring. Native peoples ate the berries fresh or mixed them with grease. The berries can also be made into jams and jellies or added to baked goods. Bears eat large amounts of crowberries. **Where found:** coniferous forest floor, acidic peatlands and rocky slopes; across northern boreal forest.

Dwarf Birch

Betula pumila

Height: up to 2 m
Leaves: 1–4 cm long; oval to circular; coarsely toothed
Flowers: 12–25 mm catkins; male hanging, female erect
Fruit: small, winged nutlets

Dwarf birch is a common shrub of the boreal forest. The smooth, dark grey or reddish brown bark of older shrubs has raised pores called lenticels. The branches, with their small, attractive leaves, make a unique addition to flower arrangements. • Some Native peoples chewed the stems then packed the poultice into deep cuts to stop bleeding. Boiling the leaves and branches into tea was said to aid in weight loss, and tea made from the cones was used to relieve menstrual cramps. **Where found:** marshes, sloughs, bogs; boreal forest. **Also known as:** swamp birch.

Beaked Hazelnut

Corylus cornuta

Height: up to 3 m
Leaves: 5–10 cm long; elliptical, heart-shaped or round base
Flowers: in catkins; male hanging, 4–7 cm; female tiny, crimson
Fruit: spherical nuts, 2–3 cm long

Plentiful, edible wild hazelnuts are rich in protein, but sometimes become infested with grubs just when they are ready to harvest. A bristly, greenish, beaked husk surrounds each round nut. Nuts may be single or in groups of 2 or 3. They can be roasted and eaten whole or ground into flour. • If you have sharp eyes, you may spot the hazelnut's tiny, crimson female flowers in spring. **Where found:** moist, well-drained woodlands; southern boreal forest, parkland.

Sweet Gale

Myrica gale

Height: to 2 m
Leaves: 6 cm long; lance-shaped, upper third of leaf toothed
Flowers: to 1.5 cm long; yellowish green, waxy catkins
Fruit: oval nutlets, 3 mm long in 8 mm long, cone-like catkins

These unusual plants bear flowers of only one sex each year, alternating between bearing female flowers one year, then male flowers the next. This nitrogen-fixing plant can survive where other plants cannot. • Sweet gale has a long history of varied uses. Long before hops was introduced, sweet gale was used to flavour English ale. Native peoples boiled buds and bark into a yellow dye for colouring porcupine quills and tanning leather. This aromatic plant can freshen linens and repel household insects. Today, sweet gale remains in demand in the aromatherapy industry. **Where found:** wet, low elevation areas such as bogs, streamsides; boreal forest, parkland.

Pussy Willow

Salix discolor

Height: up to 11 m (rarely taller)
Leaves: 3–10 cm long; somewhat variable, ellipti-cal, wavy-edged
Flowers: tiny; on hairy catkins 2–4 cm long
Fruit: hairy capsules, 8–10 mm long

Many species of willows are in our range, and many are tough to iden-tify. With its hairy felt-like catkins, pussy willow is common and distinc-tive. • Many butterfly species, including the mourning cloak, use willow as the larval host plant. Growing quickly with exten-sive root systems, willows are good for erosion control and revegetating burned areas. • The stems of some species are used for wickerwork or, traditionally, for dream-catcher charms. The wet inner bark fibres were twisted into fishing nets and ropes. The hollow stems were used as drinking straws or for making pipes. Green branches can be used to smoke meat. **Where found:** moist to wet open sites; southern boreal forest, parkland.

Red-osier Dogwood

Cornus sericea

Height: 50 cm–3 m
Leaves: 2–10 cm long; egg- or lance-shaped
Flowers: 5 mm across; white, in dense, flat-topped clusters
Fruit: white, berry-like drupes, 5–7 mm across

This attractive, hardy, deciduous shrub has distinctive
purple to red branches with white flowers in spring, red
leaves in autumn and white, berry-like drupes in winter.
The opposite leaves have 5–7 prominent veins. Dogwood
is easily grown from cuttings and makes an interesting addition to a native plant
garden. • Native peoples smoked the dried inner bark alone or mixed it with
tobacco or common bearberry leaves. The flexible branches can be woven into
baskets. **Where found:** moist sites; southern two-thirds of SK/MB.

Alder-leaved Buckthorn

Rhamnus alnifonia

Height: <1 m
Leaves: 3–10 cm long; lance- to egg-shaped
Flowers: 3 mm; yellowish green
Fruit: reddish to blue-black, berry-like drupes, 6–8 mm

Alder-leaved buckthorn has tapered leaves with
6–8 prominent, nearly straight veins and clusters of
small flowers. • **Caution:** All parts of this plant,
including the berries, contain glycosides that can cause vomiting and diarrhea. Raccoons, grey catbirds and brown thrashers
are able to eat the fruit. • The species name *alnifolia* means "alder-like leaves" and
stems from the Latin words *alnus* ("alder") and *folium* ("leaf"). **Where found:**
moist, shady woods; boreal forest, parkland.

Cloudberry

Rubus chamaemorus

Height: 5–20 cm
Leaves: 2–7 cm across; round to kidney-shaped, 5–7 lobed
Flowers: 1–2 cm across; white
Fruit: amber to reddish drupelets, 15 mm across, in raspberry-like clusters

There is something magical about cloudberries, perhaps that the luscious,
golden yellow berries seem to float above the stems or perhaps that something so juicy
can be borne out of the tundra. These raspberry-like "berries" were an important fruit
for northern Native peoples, second only to blueberries. The fruit was eaten fresh or
preserved in grease, and the leaves were used to stretch tobacco supplies. • Fresh cloudberries should be eaten right away, before they become mushy. They also make delicious jams, jellies and wine. **Where found:** boreal wetlands, sphagnum bogs, moist
tundra; boreal forest, northern SK/MB. **Also known as:** bake-apple.

Wild Red Raspberry

Rubus idaeus

Height: 1–2 m
Leaves: 4–8 cm long; compound, with 3–5 toothed leaves
Flowers: 8–12 mm wide; white, 5 petals
Fruit: red raspberries (druplets), 1 cm across

Delicious, plump raspberries can be eaten straight off the bush or made into jams, jellies or pies. Tender young shoots may be eaten raw once the prickly outer layer has been peeled off. Fresh or completely dried leaves make excellent tea, but wilted leaves can be toxic. • Traditionally, raspberry-leaf tea was given to women to treat painful menstruation or during childbirth to reduce labour pains, increase milk flow or aid in recovery. • Dwarf raspberry (*R. pubescens*) hugs the ground in wet areas across the boreal forest, bearing a single red raspberry. **Where found:** thickets, clearings, open woods; throughout except tundra.

Prickly Wild Rose

Rosa acicularis

Height: 20cm –1.2 m
Leaves: compound, 3–9 oblong leaflets, each 2–5 cm long
Flowers: 5–7 cm across; showy, pink
Fruit: red hips, about 15 mm long

These sweet-smelling deciduous shrubs, with their fragrant pink roses and scarlet, berry-like hips are widespread across our region. The stems are covered with many small bristles. • Most parts of rose shrubs are edible, but the sweet, nutritious hips, rich in vitamin C, are eaten most commonly. Avoid the seeds; their sliver-like hairs can irritate the digestive tract and cause "itchy bum." • Common wild rose or wood rose (*R. woodsii*) has fewer, scattered thorns, usually at stem nodes. **Where found:** dry to moist sites; throughout.

Shrubby Cinquefoil

Dasiphora fruticosa

Height: up to 1–1.5 m tall
Leaves: 2 cm long; pinnately compound, 3–7 (usually 5) leaflets
Flowers: 2–3 cm wide; yellow, saucer-shaped, single in leaf axils or in small clusters at branch tips
Fruit: tiny; egg-shaped, hairy achenes

Commonly planted in parking lot islands, shrubby cinquefoil is a common garden ornamental with many cultivars. In the wild, it often indicates high-quality habitats.
• Traditionally, the leaves were used to spice meat and were boiled into a tea that was in high calcium. Medicinal teas, made of the leaves, stems and roots, have mild astringent properties and were used to treat congestion, tuberculosis and fevers. **Where found:** wet prairie, fens, rocky shores; throughout.

Narrow-leaved Meadowsweet

Spiraea alba

Height: up to 1.5 m
Leaves: 3–6 cm; narrow, elliptical
Flowers: 5–8 mm; white, in long, dense clusters
Fruit: clusters of small pods

Narrow-leaved meadowsweet's tall, pyramid-shaped flower clusters appear throughout the summer. The flower clusters look slightly fuzzy because they are covered in fine hairs. Mature branches have purplish grey, peeling bark. • The leaves of this plant were traditionally steeped into a flavourful tea. **Where found:** moist sandy or rocky sites, riparian areas, lakeshores, ditches; throughout except extreme north. **Also known as:** white meadowsweet.

159

Bristly Black Currant

Ribes lacustre

Height: 50 cm–1.5 m
Leaves: 3–4 cm wide; maple-like, 3–5 pointed lobes
Flowers: 1.3 mm long petals; reddish, saucer-shaped, in clusters of 7–15
Fruit: bristly, black berries, 6 mm across

Almost 30 species of native currants and gooseberries are found across Canada. All are edible, but flavour varies greatly with species, habitat and season. The fruit may be eaten raw, cooked or dried. Currants are high in pectin and make excellent jams and jellies. Mixed with other berries, they are used to flavour liqueurs or make wines. Small mammals and birds also consume currants. The spines of bristly black currant can cause an allergic reaction in some people • Wild currants are the intermediate host for blister rust, a virulent disease of native 5-needled pines. **Where found:** moist, wooded or open sites; throughout.

Skunk Currant

Ribes glandulosum

Height: up to 1 m
Leaves: 2–7 cm across; maple-like with 5–7 lobes
Flowers: 6 mm; yellowish green, in clusters of 6–15
Fruit: bristly, red berries, 6 mm across

The crushed leaves and stems of this plant emit a distinct, skunk-like odour. • The bristly red berries are not very palatable but are eaten by moose, chipmunks, martens and birds, including thrushes, thrashers and waxwings. Raw currants tend to be very tart, but these common shrubs provide a safe emergency food source. • Several other *Ribes* species (currants and gooseberries) are found in various habitats throughout SK/MB. All have leaves shaped like maple leaves, with 3–5 lobes (occasionally 7) and red or black berries. **Where found:** damp forests, swampy areas, clearings; throughout to tundra.

Canada Buffaloberry

Shepherdia canadensis

Height: 1–3 m
Leaves: 2–6 cm long; elliptical, greenish above, silvery below
Flowers: 4 mm wide; greenish yellow
Fruit: bright red, oval berry, 4–6 mm

This deciduous shrub has dark green leaves that are silvery below with star-shaped hairs and rust-coloured scales. The tempting, juicy, translucent red berries are quite sour, but many Native peoples enjoyed them. • Buffaloberries contain a bitter, soapy substance (saponin) that foams when beaten. They were whipped like egg whites to make a foamy "ice-cream" dessert, which was sweetened with other berries and, later, with sugar. **Where found:** open woods, streambanks; boreal forest, parkland. **Also known as:** soapberry.

Wolf Willow

Elaeagnus commutata

Height: 1–3 m
Leaves: 3–8 cm long; silvery grey, oval-shaped
Flowers: 3 mm across; yellowish green, funnel-shaped
Fruit: silvery, dry, mealy berry, 6 mm wide

This beautiful silvery shrub flowers in June, giving off a sweet, musky scent. Flowering dates of wolf willow can be reported to PlantWatch, a national volunteer program that helps scientists track changes in the environment. • The dry, astringent berries of this plant (known as "silverberries") were traditionally only eaten in times of famine. More commonly, the beautifully striped, stony seeds inside the berries were cleaned, oiled and polished, then used as decorative beads. **Where found:** edge habitats, dry hillsides, open areas; throughout to tundra. **Also known as:** silverberry.

Silver Sagebrush

Artemisia cana

Height: 40 cm–1.25 cm
Leaves: 1–4 cm long; elliptical, silvery, hairy
Flowers: minute; yellowish green
Fruit: small achenes

These common shrubs, true prairie plants, have a sage-like aroma and greyish, shredding bark. Green, leafy branches were traditionally burned as ceremonial smudges to cleanse participants of impurities and evil spirits, and they are still used in this way today. Sagebrush has been used in a wide variety of medicines and its extracts are reputed to kill many types of bacteria, but some classify this plant as toxic. The aromatic, volatile oils have been used in shampoos and as insect repellents. **Where found:** uplands, overgrazed areas; southern parkland, prairie.

Common Rabbitbrush

Chrysothamnus nauseosus

Height: to 1.3 m
Leaves: 1–5 cm long; thin, thread-like, grey-green
Flowers: 12 mm across; bright yellow, in a cluster
Fruit: slender, hairy achene

The milky sap of these shrubs contains latex (rubbery compounds). The bark and roots of rabbitbrush were traditionally used as chewing gum, though the toxicity of these plants remains uncertain, so chewing or eating these plants is not recommended. • Native peoples boiled the bright yellow flowers to produce a lemon-yellow dye. Immature buds or twigs produce a greenish yellow dye. **Where found:** dry prairie, eroded hillsides; southern SK.

Labrador Tea

Ledum groenlandicum

Height: 30–80 cm
Leaves: 1–5 cm long; oblong, leather, rusty below
Flowers: 5–8 mm across; white, in umbrella-shaped clusters
Fruit: dry, drooping capsules, 5–7 mm long

This evergreen shrub saves energy by keeping its leaves year round. The leaves have a thick, leathery texture, rolled edges and distinctive rusty-coloured, woolly hairs on their undersides, all adaptations that help the plant conserve moisture. Labrador tea may also produce chemicals that discourage other plants from growing nearby. • First Nations peoples and early settlers made the leaves and flowers into a tea that was rich in vitamin C. **Caution:** Consuming large amounts can be toxic; do not confuse this plant with other poisonous heaths such as bog laurel or bog rosemary. **Where found:** moist, acidic, nutrient-poor soils, often associated with black spruce; boreal forest, parkland.

Bearberry

Arctostaphylos uva-ursi

Height: to 10 cm
Leaves: 1–3 cm long; dark green, oval, leathery
Flowers: 4–6 mm wide; pinkish, urn-shaped
Fruit: dull red, berry-like drupes, 6–10 mm across

Thick, leathery evergreen leaves help this common, mat-forming shrub survive on dry, sunny slopes where others would perish. Trailing branches that may be up to 1 m long send down roots, and the flowers nod in small clusters. • The red "berries" are edible but are rather mealy and tasteless. They were traditionally cooked and mixed with grease or fish eggs to reduce their dryness. • The glossy leaves were widely used for smoking, both alone and later with tobacco. **Where found:** sandy, well-drained, open or wooded sites; throughout except grasslands. **Also known as:** kinnikinnick.

Velvet Leaf Blueberry

Vaccinium myrtilloides

Height: 10–50 cm
Leaves: 1–4 cm long; oblong to eliptical
Flowers: 3–5 mm wide; greenish white, in clusters
Fruit: blue berries, 4–8 mm across

Plentiful blueberries were the most important fruits for northern Native peoples, and blueberry picking remains a favourite family tradition today. Traditionally the berries were eaten fresh, dried or preserved in grease. The roots and stems were boiled into various medicinal teas, used for headaches, to regulate menstruation or even prevent pregnancy (stems). Today, young and old alike enjoy blueberry pie, jam, pancakes and even blueberry wine. **Where found:** sandy soils in forests and clearings; parkland, boreal forest. **Also known as:** huckleberry.

Lingonberry

Vaccinium vitis-idaea

Height: 10–20 cm, creeping
Leaves: 6–15 mm long; leathery, elliptic to oval
Flowers: 5 mm long; pinkish cups
Fruit: red berry, 5–10 mm wide

In northern regions, mixed patches of lingonberry, lichen and Labrador tea carpet the ground in a mosaic of reddish brown. The smooth, dark green leaves have dark spots on their undersides. • The lingonberry was the third most important fruit to northern Native peoples, after blueberry and cloudberry. The acidic berries were usually collected after the first frost and were commonly used in pemmican or cooked with grease, fish or meat. Berries were boiled into a dye for porcupine quills or dried as beads for necklaces. **Where found:** various habitats, bogs, rocky barrens, moist areas, dry woods; boreal forest,tundra. **Also known as:** bog cranberry.

Leatherleaf

Chamaedaphne calyculata

Height: up to 1 m
Leaves: 1–4 cm long; lance-shaped or elliptic, leathery
Flowers: 5–6 mm across; white, urn-shaped, in clusters
Fruit: brownish capsules, up to 6 mm long

Leatherleaf is a genuine bog species that can be found in almost every boreal bog. This low evergreen shrub forms patches of dense thickets or floating mats at the edges of lakes or swamps. Its delicate, urn-shaped flowers grow in long clusters, then give way to fruit capsules that contain abundant tiny seeds. **Where found:** wet coniferous bogs and swamps, lakeshores; parkland, boreal forest.

Dwarf Bog Rosemary

Andromeda polifolia

Height: 10–40 cm
Leaves: 1–5 cm long; dull green, leathery, oblong
Flowers: 6 mm across; white-pinkish, urn-shaped
Fruit: small, round capsules, 6 mm wide

Despite resembling and sharing the name of a common kitchen herb, bog rosemary contains poisonous andromedotoxin compounds that can cause breathing problems, vomiting and even death if ingested. • The leathery leaves of this plant curl under, and their undersides are covered with fine hairs to help prevent moisture loss. • Bog rosemary has rounded stems and bluish green, alternate leaves, unlike bog laurel *(Kalmia polifolia)*, which has flattened stems and shiny, green, opposite leaves. **Where found:** wet areas, coniferous swamps, sphagnum bogs, lakeshores; throughout except grasslands.

Prince's Pine

Chimaphila umbellata

Height: 10–30 cm
Leaves: 2–8 cm long; elliptical, toothed, leathery
Flowers: <1 cm across; white to pinkish, bell-shaped
Fruit: rounded capsules, 5–7 mm across

The leaves of this semi-woody, evergreen shrub are dark, glossy green above and pale beneath. The flowers are waxy, and the fruits are round capsules. This attractive plant needs certain soil fungi to live and often dies when transplanted, so it is best enjoyed in the wild. • Prince's pine has been used to flavour candy, soft drinks (especially root beer) and traditional beers. Several Native groups smoked the dried leaves. **Where found:** wooded, usually coniferous sites; boreal forest. **Also known as:** pipsissewa.

Twinflower

Linnaea borealis

Height: 3–10 cm; loose mats, erect branches
Leaves: 1–2 cm long; evergreen, oval
Flowers: 3–10 cm tall; pairs of pink bells, trumpet-like
Fruit: dry nutlets, 2–3 mm wide

This trailing, semi-woody evergreen is an excellent native ground cover in partially shaded sites. The small, delicate pairs of pink bells are easily overlooked among other plants on the forest floor, but their strong, sweet perfume may draw you to them in the evening. Hooked bristles on the tiny, egg-shaped nutlets catch on fur, feathers or clothing of passersby, who then carry these inconspicuous hitchhikers to new locations. **Where found:** moist, open or shaded sites; throughout except grasslands.

Common Snowberry

Symphoricarpos albus

Height: 50–75 cm
Leaves: 2–4 cm long; oval
Flowers: 4–7 mm long; pink to white, bell-shaped
Fruit: white, berry-like, 6–10 mm long

The name "snowberry" refers to the waxy, white, berry-like drupes that remain in small clusters near branch tips through winter. • **Caution:** All parts of this deciduous shrub are toxic and will cause vomiting and diarrhea. • Some Native groups called the fruits "corpse berries," because they were believed to be the ghosts of saskatoons—part of the spirit world, not to be eaten by the living. • The broadly funnel-shaped flowers are pink to white and have hairy centres. • The closely related western snowberry (*S. occidentalis*) has thicker, oblong leaves and clusters of greenish white berries. **Where found:** well-drained sites; boreal forest, parkland. **Also known as:** waxberry.

Nannyberry

Viburnum lentago

Height: 4–7 m
Leaves: 5–10 cm long; elliptical with round base
Flowers: 4–8 mm across; white, in flat-topped clusters
Fruit: berry-like drupes, 8–12 mm across

Fragrant flowers, showy, bluish black fruit and reddish winter twigs make nannyberry a popular ornamental. It responds well to pruning, but the suckering roots can sometimes prove troublesome. • The edible fruit tastes like raisins and can be eaten raw or used in jams and jellies. Many wild birds, including wild turkeys, grouse and songbirds, feed on the fruit, then disperse the seeds. **Where found:** wet, rich sites near water, roadsides, thickets; southern half of SK/MB.

Highbush Cranberry

Viburnum opulus var. americanum

Height: up to 4 m
Leaves: 5–11 cm long; 3 pointed, spreading lobes
Flowers: 1–2 cm wide; white, in flat-topped clusters
Fruit: orange to red berry-like drupes, 1 cm across

Shiny, red to orange highbush cranberry fruit makes a tart, tasty trailside snack and is easy to pick for use in jams and jellies. The berry-like fruits remain above the snow in winter. Raw fruits should not be eaten in large quantities because they can cause vomiting and severe cramps. • Several *Viburnums* grow in our area, including lowbush cranberry (*V. edule*), which is found in moist habitats, wetland margins and steamsides. **Where found:** moist, rich sites near water in cool woodlands; northern parkland, southern boreal forest.

Bracted Honeysuckle

Lonicera involucrata

Height: 1–3 m, climbing vine
Leaves: 5–10 cm long; lance-shaped, hairy
Flowers: in pairs, yellow, tubular, cupped by 1–2 cm long, purplish bracts
Fruit: in pairs, purplish black berries, 8 mm across

The unusual, shiny berries of these deciduous shrubs, with their broad, spreading, backward-bending, shiny red to purplish bracts, catch the eyes of passersby and also of hungry bears and birds. **Caution:** Despite their tempting appearance, these berries are unpalatable, and they can be toxic. • Many other honeysuckles occur in our region. Twining honeysuckle (*L. dioica* var. *glaucescens*) has oval leaves and yellow-orange, funnel-shaped flowers. **Where found:** moist to wet, usually shaded sites; throughout to tundra.

White Clematis

Clematis ligusticifolia

Height: up to 6 m, climbing vine
Leaves: paired, divided into 5–7 leaflets, each 3–6 cm long
Flowers: 2 cm across; creamy white, star-shaped
Fruit: small achenes with long, feathery bristles

With its eye-catching cream-coloured flower clusters and large, fluffy seedheads, this woody-stemmed vine makes an excellent ornamental. Flowers appear in late July. Propagated from seed or by layering sections of vine, white clematis grows best in sunny spots where the plant base is shaded. It is a common roadside species. • Another common native species, purple clematis (*C. verticellaris*) bears long, 4-petalled, star-like flowers in June. **Where found:** moist to dry, open sites; prairie, southern parkland. **Also known as:** western clematis.

Poison Ivy

Toxicodendron radicans

Height: to 1 m, groundcover, shrublet or climbing vine
Leaves: 4–10 cm long; compound, 3 leaflets
Flowers: 1–3 mm across; greenish white
Fruit: white berries, 5 mm across

This species is the one plant that anyone venturing outdoors should learn. Identification difficulties are compounded by its variable growth habit: trailing groundcover, small erect shrublet or vine climbing high into trees or on other objects. A brush with this plant can cause a severe allergic reaction, obvious in an itchy rash and swelling. To hyper-responders, contact can even be life threatening. The rash can sometimes be alleviated by washing with plenty of soap, but if symptoms worsen, seek medical attention. • Poison ivy is actually rather showy, especially in autumn when leaflets turn red and ripe berries become white. Many species of birds eat the fruit. **Where found:** opportunistic, various dry to moist upland sites; southern SK/MB.

FORBS, FERNS & GRASSES

orbs are non-woody, seed-bearing plants—essentially all broad-leaved plants that are not ferns, grasses, sedges, or trees or shrubs. They are often perennials that grow from a persistent rootstock, but many are short-lived annuals. A great variety of plants are forbs, including all our spring wildflowers, prairie sunflowers, many flowering wetland plants, herbs used in gardening for food or medicine and numerous weeds. Many herbs are used for adding flavour to foods and in herbal remedies, aromatherapy and dyes. Culinary herbs are typically made from the leaves of non-woody plants, but medicinal herbs may be made from flowers, fruit, seeds, bark or roots of both non-woody and woody plants. Various forbs also flower into unique, delicate and beautiful colours and forms. They are the inspiration of artists and poets and are often symbols of romance, or have meanings attached to them through folklore, legend or superstition. Forbs are also vital to the ecology of the plant communities in which they occur as food sources for pollinating insects and other animals, host plants for moths and butterflies, nest material for birds and cover for many animal species.

The forbs illustrated here are but the most frequent and likely to be seen examples. Saskatchewan and Manitoba host hundreds of species of native forbs; far more than we could hope to include. The species we have included should provide a good starting point for those wishing to delve further into the spectacular and diverse flora of our region.

Orchids
p. 169

Irises
p. 169

Lilies
pp. 169–71

Knotweed
p. 171

Nettles
p. 172

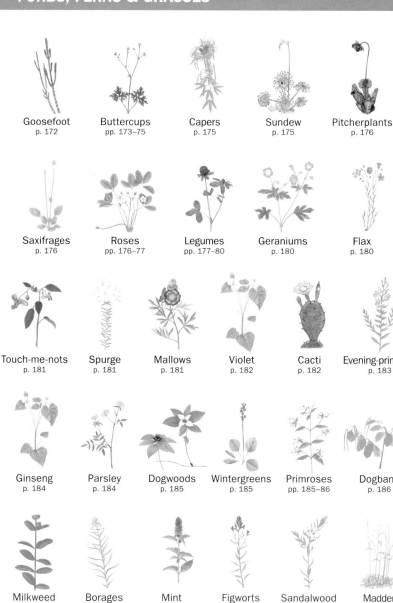

Goosefoot
p. 172

Buttercups
pp. 173–75

Capers
p. 175

Sundew
p. 175

Pitcherplants
p. 176

Saxifrages
p. 176

Roses
pp. 176–77

Legumes
pp. 177–80

Geraniums
p. 180

Flax
p. 180

Touch-me-nots
p. 181

Spurge
p. 181

Mallows
p. 181

Violet
p. 182

Cacti
p. 182

Evening-primrose
p. 183

Ginseng
p. 184

Parsley
p. 184

Dogwoods
p. 185

Wintergreens
p. 185

Primroses
pp. 185–86

Dogbane
p. 186

Milkweed
p. 186

Borages
p. 187

Mint
pp. 187–88

Figworts
pp. 188–89

Sandalwood
p. 189

Madder
p. 190

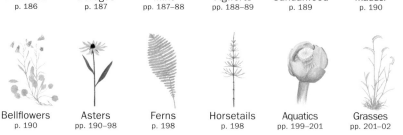

Bellflowers
p. 190

Asters
pp. 190–98

Ferns
p. 198

Horsetails
p. 198

Aquatics
pp. 199–201

Grasses
pp. 201–02

Yellow Lady's-slipper

Cypripedium parviflorum

Height: 10–70 cm
Leaves: to 20 cm long; lance-shaped
Flowers: 4 twisted petals around a yellow, 3.5 cm long, sac-like pouch
Fruit: oblong capsules, to 25 mm long, release tiny seeds

Finding any of our native orchids is always a treat. The large, sac-like flowers are adapted for pollination by large bumblebees. The plants depend on special mycorrhzal fungi for nutrient intake, water absorption and seed growth. Do not transplant these unusual orchids—they will likely not survive without the fungi. • Other uncommon but showy orchids include rattlesnake-plantain (*Goodyera repens*) and various bog orchids (*Habenaria* spp). They have white or greenish flowers on an extended spike. **Where found:** cool, wet soil of bogs, riparian areas; boreal forest, parkland; scattered and local.

Common Blue-eyed Grass

Sisyrinchium montanum

Height: 10–50 cm
Leaves: 1–3.5 mm wide; grass-like
Flowers: 8–10 mm long; blue to violet, 6 pointed tepals, yellow eye
Fruit: black capsules, 3–6 mm long

The dainty blue flowers of this wildflower add fleeting beauty to damp meadows and woodland trails. Common blue-eyed grass is not a true grass but a member of the iris family. If you compare the stems, you'll find that the stems of these plants are flat or 2-sided, not round like the stems of grasses. • Dozens of blue-eyed grass species are found around the world, but some have white, yellow or purple flowers. These beautiful flowers have been much reduced by people picking them or transplanting as garden plants. They're best enjoyed by leaving them where they grow. **Where found:** moist, open areas; throughout.

Wood Lily

Lilium philadelphicum

Height: 30–70 cm
Leaves: 3–10 cm long; lance-shaped, whorled
Flowers: 6–10 cm wide; orange tepals with purplish dotted throats, goblet-shaped
Fruit: erect, cylindrical capsules, 2–4 cm long

The most shockingly brilliant orange flowers of wood lilies spring up along roadsides and in woodlands across much of Canada. • Don't dig these plants out of the ground! Picking the flowers can kill the entire plant, and overzealous collectors have caused lilies to disappear in places. • Western red lily (var. *andinum*) is the provincial emblem of Saskatchewan. **Where found:** roadsides, dry woods, meadows; boreal forest and southward.

Wild Lily-of-the-Valley

Maianthemum canadense

Height: 15 cm
Leaves: 2–8 cm long; 2 per plant
Flowers: 4–6 mm wide; white, star-shaped, in erect clusters
Fruit: red berry, 4–6 mm wide

This small understorey herb has 2 (occasionally 3) leaves with parallel-veins and heart-shaped bases. Native peoples used the leaves to promote healing, crushing the plant into a poultice to treat cuts, minor burns and sore eyes. • The berries are brownish green and turn red when ripe. The red or green berries are edible, but their taste is unremarkable. Beware—too many can cause diarrhea. **Where found:** moist woodlands; boreal forest and southward.

Starry False Solomon's-seal

Maianthemum stellatum

Height: 15–60 cm
Leaves: 3–12 cm long; elliptical, prominent veins
Flowers: 6 mm wide; white, in spike-like clusters
Fruit: greenish berry with brown stripes, <1 cm wide

False Solomon's-seal is easily told from true Solomon's-seal (*Polygonatum* spp.) by the flower arrangement. In this species, the flowers form a plume at the terminus of the leaves; in true Solomon's-seal the flowers dangle in small clusters under the leaves. The species name *stellatum,* from the Latin *stella* for "star," describes the white flowers with 6 petals and 6 sepals. The boldly striped fruit darkens to reddish black with age. **Where found:** moist to dry sites; boreal forest and southward. **Previously known as:** *Smilacina stellata.*

Prairie Onion

Allium textile

Height: to 50 cm
Leaves: 10–15 cm long; thin, basal leaves
Flowers: 5–7 mm long; white, in clusters of 8–20
Fruit: oblong capsules, 4 mm wide

When their flowers are not displayed, wild onions can be distinguished from poisonous relatives, such as white death-camas, by their strong onion smell. Do not try the taste test. • Many Native groups enjoyed wild onions as a vegetable and as flavouring in other foods. Bears, ground squirrels, and marmots also enjoy wild onions. • The thick bulbs are 3-lobed capsules with netted outer layers. **Where found:** dry, open sites; prairie, parkland.

White Death-camas

Zygadenus elegans

Height: 20–60 cm
Leaves: up to 1.2 cm long
Flowers: 7–12 mm wide
Fruit: capsules, 1.5 cm wide

This perennial contains the poisonous alkaloid zygadenine, which some people claim is more potent than strychnine. Death-camas has been confused with wild onions, blue camas, white hyacinth and fritillarias, with disastrous results. When in doubt, spit it out! If ingested, induce vomiting and get medical help. • Growing from blackish scaly bulbs, this plant has pale, foul-smelling flowers, each with 6 greenish, heart-shaped glands near the centre. The fruits are erect, 3-lobed capsules. **Where found:** moist, open sites; parkland, prairie.

Yellow Umbrellaplant

Eriogonum flavum

Height: 10–20 cm, occasionally to 40 cm
Leaves: 3–5 cm long; basal, paddle-shaped, felted
Flowers: 12 mm wide; pale yellow, in flat-topped clusters
Fruit: tiny; hairy seed-like achenes

Yellow umbrellaplant's delicate, modest flowers have a strong scent that may be unpleasant to humans but is irresistible to bees and other insects. Several flat-topped flower clusters appear at once, creating a showy display that attracts pollinators. The thick-felted leaves retain moisture. **Where found:** dry, eroded areas, hillsides, badlands; prairie, grasslands. **Also known as:** golden wild-buckwheat, sulphur plant.

Western Dock

Rumex occidentalis

Height: 50 cm–1.5 m
Leaves: 5–20 cm long; lance-shaped with heart-shaped bases
Flowers: dense, 10–40 cm long clusters; greenish to reddish
Fruit: papery achenes, 2–4 mm long

Edible dock leaves are a good source of protein, calcium, iron, potassium and vitamins A and C. Raw leaves may be bitter, but cooked leaves add a lemony zing to soups or stews. Dock leaves, like those of the closely related beet (*Beta vulgaris*), contain oxalic acid, which is safe in moderation but toxic if consumed in large quantities. • Several *Rumex* species grow in our region. Curled dock (*R. crispus*) is an introduced, weedy species found in prairies and parkland. **Where found:** moist, often disturbed ground; throughout.

Stinging Nettle

Urtica dioica

Height: 50 cm–2 m
Leaves: 4–15 cm long; coarsely toothed
Flowers: 1–2 mm long; green to purplish, in drooping clusters
Fruit: achenes, 1–2 mm long

The stinging hairs on the stems and undersides of this plant's leaves contain formic acid and can cause itching and burning. The sting lasts 10 minutes to several days, depending on how sensitive you are.
• Some people use gloves to pick young, tender nettles to make soup or steam them as a delicious spring vegetable. Cooking destroys the acid, but eating large amounts may cause irritation. **Where found:** moist, rich meadows, ditches, woodlands, disturbed sites; throughout.

Strawberry Blite

Chenopodium capitatum

Height: to 50 cm
Leaves: 3–7 cm long; broadly spear-shaped, coarsely toothed
Flowers: minute; green, in strawberry-shaped clusters
Fruit: thin achenes

The genus *Chenopodium* includes several plants of minor to moderate importance as food crops, including quinoa (*C. quinoa),* canihua (*C. pallidicaule)* and lamb's-quarters (*C. album*). The nutritious leaves contain significant amounts of protein, fibre, calcium, phosphorus, iron and vitamins A and C. Leaves may be eaten raw in small amounts (large quantities can cause photosensitivity) but are best cooked or steamed and served like spinach. First Nations recognized the vitamin C content and ate the leaves to prevent scurvy. **Caution:** saponins in the seeds are potentially toxic. Leaves contain toxic oxalic acids, but these are mainly removed by cooking. **Where found:** roadsides, cultivated fields, throughout.

Red Saltwort

Salicornia rubra

Height: to 25 cm
Leaves: 3 mm long; dark reddish, scale-like
Flowers: minute; scale-like
Fruit: small, flattened seed

Sodium chloride (common table salt) is poisonous to most plants. Red saltwort has adapted to saline conditions by integrating salt into its tissues to balance the osmotic pressures exerted by environmental concentrations. Consequently, the plant is very salty to taste and can be dried and ground into a powdery salt substitute. Young shoots make excellent pickles after boiling them in their own salted water. Only the top 10 cm should be collected, leaving the bottom to produce new shoots. **Where found:** saline sloughs, dry marshes; southern grasslands.

Prairie Crocus

Pulsatilla patens

Height: to 10 cm high (stems)
Leaves: 4–10 cm wide; basal, grey-green, much divided
Flowers: 4 cm wide; blue to mauve, petal-like bracts covered in woolly hairs
Fruit: feathery achenes on a long stalk

This low, furry plant appears early in spring and blooms right after the snow melts. Leaves appear as the flowers fade. • True crocuses are part of the lily family, but prairie crocuses are related to anemones and are part of the buttercup family. • Prairie crocus is the provincial flower of Manitoba. **Where found:** dry, open woods, sandy soils, prairie; throughout except taiga shield. **Also known as:** pasqueflower. **Previously known as:** *Anemone patens.*

Canada Anemone

Anemone canadensis

Height: 20–70 cm
Leaves: 5–15 cm long; 3–5 deep lobes
Flowers: 2–4 cm across; white
Fruit: seed-like achenes, 3–5 mm, clustered in round heads

Beautiful, delicate Canada anemone flowers bloom white in June and July, unfolding above unique, deeply lobed leaves. The flowers do not have true petals, but 5 showy, petal-like sepals. Small, green seed clusters (achenes) appear after the blooms fade. • "Anemone" comes from the Greek word for "wind"; these plants are also called windflowers. It was once thought that the flowers only bloomed on windy spring days. **Where found:** moist, open sites, roadsides, gravely shores; throughout but most common in prairie-parkland.

Yellow Marsh-marigold

Caltha palustris

Height: 20–60 cm
Leaves: 5–17 cm wide; basal, heart-shaped or kidney-shaped, toothed
Flowers: 15–40 mm across; 5–9 yellow sepals surround numerous stamen
Fruit: follicle with red seeds, 10–15 mm long

One of spring's great botanical spectacles is a mass blooming of these gorgeous buttercups in swampy woods. Early wildflowers, marsh-marigolds have come and gone by the time spring's procession of wildflowers reaches peak abundance. To humans, these flowers look evenly yellow, but insects can detect distinct ultraviolet light patterns along the petals that guide them to the centre of the flower. **Caution:** raw leaves contain a toxin that can irritate skin and is poisonous if eaten. **Where found:** swampy woods, sometimes wet meadows, bogs, fens; throughout.

Meadow Buttercup

Ranunculus acris

Height: 60 cm–1 m
Leaves: 5 cm wide, palmately 3–5 lobed, basal
Flowers: 2.5 cm across; bright yellow, 5 petals
Fruit: smooth, round achenes

Pretty yellow buttercups flower over deeply parted, palmate leaves. • Buttercups are named for the toxic ranunculin contained in their sap. It causes symptoms that include dermatitis, mouth blisters and intense burning pain of the digestive tract when ingested. Drying and cooking are said to degrade the poison, rendering plants or hay containing buttercups harmless. **Where found:** disturbed ground, fields; boreal forest, parkland.

Red Baneberry

Actaea rubra

Height: 30 cm–1 m
Leaves: 2–10 cm long; divided 2–3 times into groups of 3 leaflets
Flowers: 7 mm across; white
Fruit: glossy, red or white berries, 6–8 mm long

This perennial has long-stalked, rounded clusters of white flowers, each with 5–10 tiny, slender petals. • **Caution:** Although birds and small mammals eat the tempting, glossy, red or white berries, baneberry is toxic to humans. As few as 2 berries can cause cramps, headaches, vomiting, bloody diarrhea and/or dizziness. • Some Native peoples considered baneberry to be sacred and used it in religious ceremonies, but this plant was always treated with respect, because it could kill the user. **Where found:** moist, often shady sites; throughout.

Wild Columbine

Aquilegia canadensis

Height: up to 60 cm
Leaves: to 6 cm long; mostly basal, compound, 3 leaflets with 3 lobed, rounded tips
Flowers: 3 cm long; nodding, tubular, 5 yellow petals with 4 red spurs
Fruit: 5-parted , slightly spreading pod (follicle).

A striking member of the buttercup family, columbine grows best on rocky outcrops. The colourful flowers entice hummingbirds and long-tongued butterflies, which then pollinate the plants. The entire flower is edible and decorative in salads. • The common name means "dove" and the Latin name *Aquilegia* means "eagle." Both names refer to the yellow, talon-like spurs of the flowers. • Blue-and-white flowered columbines include the native small-flowered columbine (*A. brevistyla*), and the introduced European columbine (*A. vulgaris*), which occasionally jumps the garden wall and escapes to the wild. **Where found:** moist, rocky meadows, forest openings, clearings; throughout.

Meadowrue

Thalictrum spp.

Height: 20–70 cm
Leaves: 1–2 cm long; twice divided into 3s, rounded
Flowers: 2–4 mm long; greenish, in many-flowered clusters
Fruit: seed-like achenes, 3–5 mm long

Tiny meadowrue flowers appear in showy, pyramid-shaped clusters. Plants are usually either male or female. Male flowers have dangling stamens, and the less showy female flowers give way to small fruit. • Dried seeds and leaves may be used as a fragrant potpourri. Some Native peoples used these plants in love potions. **Where found:** moist prairie, thickets, open woods; boreal forest, parkland.

Beeplant

Cleome serrulata

Height: 25 cm–1 m
Leaves: 2.5–7 cm long; lance-shaped
Flowers: 1–2 cm long; pink to lavender, in a terminal cluster
Fruit: pod, 3–6 cm long

When nectar-rich beeplant flowers in August, it attracts honeybees. The pink flowers are edible, as are the spicy seeds contained within the long pods. The rest of the plant tends to have a disagreeable odour and taste. Beeplant was occasionally eaten in times of famine; it was boiled for a long time, in a change of water, to reduce the strong flavour and smell. **Where found:** open, disturbed areas; parkland, prairie.

Round-leaf Sundew

Drosera rotundifolia

Height: 5–10 cm, occasionally taller
Leaves: tiny; round, sticky, basal, on round, hairy, flattened stalks 6 cm long
Flowers: <50 mm across; pink or white, 5 petals
Fruit: capsules, <50 mm long

Like something from a horror movie, this insect-eating plant has sticky, round leaves covered in gooey, reddish hairs that attract, trap and digest prey. The hairs are tipped with the botanical equivalent of glue, and investigating insects are caught and held fast. The hairs then slowly curl in a death-grip around the victim. A secreted enzyme dissolves the prey within 48 hours, leaving only the exoskeleton. • Sundew has been made into love potions. Some farmers in the 19th century believed that "sheep and other cattell, if they do but taste [sundew], are provoked to lust." **Where found:** peaty wetlands, primarily bogs, fens; boreal forest to treeline.

Pitcher-plant

Sarracenia purpurea

Height: up to 40 cm (flower stalks)
Leaves: to 30 cm long; basal, often water-filled
Flowers: 5–7 cm wide; purplish red, solitary, nodding
Fruit: many-seeded capsules

Don't get reincarnated as an insect—you might be consumed by this carnivorous plant. The purple-streaked hollow leaves (pitchers) secrete chemicals that attract insects. Searching for a snack, the insect enters the tubular leaf. Stiff, downward-pointing hairs prevent its retreat should it realize something is amiss. It then reaches a zone of the inner leaf that is smooth and glassy, and plunges into the juice below, which is rainwater enriched with enzymes that reduce buoyancy and speed decomposition. The plant then absorbs the insect's proteins and nitrogen, which is how it gets sustenance in nutrient-poor bog soils. **Where found:** peaty bogs, fens; boreal forest, parkland.

Grass-of-Parnassus

Parnassia palustris

Height: up to 40 cm
Leaves: to 6 cm long; roundish, mostly basal, typically one smaller stem leaf
Flowers: about 1 cm wide; white with green veins, 5 petals
Fruit: 4-valved capsules, 8–12 mm long

Grass-of-parnassus does not look like a grass and is not closely related to them. It is named after a grass that grew on Mount Parnassus in Greece. Although the foliage is glossy and attractive, the flowers are the most striking aspect of this plant. White petals are boldly striped with green, and they almost glow. • Grass-of-parnassus requires the specialized wet alkaline soils of fens, a habitat that has largely been destroyed in many areas. **Where found:** wet, calcareous seep-fed meadows or fens, roadsides, railways; parkland, prairie, grasslands.

Virginia Strawberry

Fragaria virginiana

Height: 5–15 cm
Leaves: 5–10 cm long; divided into 3 coarsely toothed leaflets
Flowers: 1.5–2 cm wide; white, 5 petals
Fruit: red strawberry dotted with tiny achenes

Few things beat running into a patch of fresh, wild strawberries. This plant is the ancestor of 90% of our culti-vated strawberries. Each tiny red berry contains all the flavour of a large domestic strawberry. The rhizomes and runners produce tufts of bluish tinged leaves with 3-toothed leaflets. **Where found:** dry fields, open woods; throughout.

Common Silverweed

Argentina anserina

Height: low, creeping
Leaves: to 30 cm long; divided into numerous toothed leaflets
Flowers: 15–25 mm across; yellow, 5 petals
Fruit: achenes, 2 mm across

This circumpolar plant carpets the ground with its sharply toothed leaflets and bright yellow flowers. The leaves, especially the undersides, are covered in silky, silver hairs, from which the plant gets its name. • Silverweed roots may be eaten raw or cooked and are said to taste like parsnips or sweet potatoes. Ground roots were traditionally steeped into medicinal tea, which was used to aid in childbirth. **Where found:** well-drained to wet, open sites including meadows, ditches and riversides; throughout except far north and southeast.

Three-flowered Avens

Geum triflorum

Height: 10–30 cm
Leaves: 5–20 cm long; mostly basal, pinnately compound, finely toothed
Flowers: 1–2 cm wide; reddish purple, nodding at end of long stem
Fruit: dense heads of feathery achenes on 3 cm long style

At first glance, a field of these plants in seed appears to be covered with low-lying haze—hence the alternate names "prairie smoke" and "old man's whisker's." This soft-hairy perennial has 3-flowered clusters of purplish to dusty-pink flowers. Each seed-like fruit has a long, feathery style that carries the fruit on the wind. • Native peoples boiled the roots to make a drink flavoured like weak sassafras tea. **Where found:** dry to moist, open sites; parkland, prairie.

Purple Prairie-clover

Dalea purpurea

Height: 30–80 cm (stems)
Leaves: divided into 3–7 leaflets, each 5–20 cm long
Flowers: 1–5 cm long; purple to rose, dense oval cluster
Fruit: small pods

Hardy purple prairie-clover is well adapted to prairie life, temperature extremes and drought. With a long, clumped, woody root system, this plant can reach for water. Small, rolled leaves also help reduce sun exposure and conserve moisture. This attractive perennial is a popular choice for restoration work and prairie gardens and is easy to grow from commercially available seed. **Where found:** dry, open sites; prairie, grasslands.

177

Alfalfa

Medicago sativa

Height: up to 1 m
Leaves: 15–30 mm long; 3 leaflets, toothed at the tip
Flowers: 6–12 mm long; purple-blue pea-like, in round clusters
Fruit: small, curved or coiled pods

Alfalfa is an important forage crop that is adaptable to a wide range of agricultural regions. Native to Iran, alfalfa was cultivated as horse feed in Greece as early as 490 BC, then imported to South America by the Spaniards. Today, this legume is harvested as hay and is often used to feed cattle. Tasty, young alfalfa sprouts are also sold as salad and a sandwich garnish. • The name alfalfa is derived from the Arabic *al-fasfasah,* meaning "best fodder." **Where found:** disturbed sites; southern boreal forest, parkland, grasslands.

Sweet-clover

Melilotus officinalis

Height: 50 cm–2 m
Leaves: 10–25 mm long; 3 leaflets, lance-shaped, toothed
Flowers: 4.5–7 mm long; yellow, pea-like, in long, narrow clusters
Fruit: pods, 3 mm long

This hardy forage crop blankets roadsides and abandoned fields in yellow, invading native grasslands and reducing diversity. Each pollinated plant can release as many as 350,000 seeds that remain viable for decades. • Sweet-clover is valued as a forage crop, soil enhancer and honey plant. The genus name stems from *meli,* Greek for "honey," and refers to this plant's abundant, nectar producing flowers. • White-flowered sweet-clover is known as *M. alba.* **Where found:** open, disturbed sites; southern boreal forest, parkland, grasslands.

Showy Locoweed

Oxytropis splendens

Height: 10–30 cm
Leaves: 5–25 cm long; basal, 7–15 lance-shaped leaflets
Flowers: 10–15 mm long; purple-blue, pea-like in dense clusters 3–10 cm long
Fruit: woolly, oval pods, 8–15 mm long

The showy flower clusters of this tufted, densely silky perennial are indeed splendid but are also dangerous. Many locoweeds contain locoine, an alkaloid that causes horses, sheep and cattle to go crazy, or "loco." • You can easily identify showy locoweed by its purplish flowers and whorled (rather than paired) leaflets. Several other locoweeds occur here, including yellow-flowered varieties. **Where found:** well-drained, usually open sites; boreal forest, parkland.

American Licorice

Glycyrrhiza lepidota

Height: 30 cm–1 m
Leaves: 2–4 cm long; 11–19 lance-shaped leaflets
Flowers: yellowish white, pea-like, in erect, 2–6 cm long clusters
Fruit: reddish brown burs, 1–2 cm long

Wild licorice has been used to flavour candy, root beer and chewing tobacco. It contains glycyrrhizin, a substance that is estimated to be 50 times sweeter than sugar and quenches (rather than increases) thirst. Wild licorice has a milder flavour but is very similar to its close European relative, licorice (*G. glabra*), from which commercial licorice is obtained. • European and Chinese species (*G. uralensis*) are among the most widely used medicinal plants in the world. Licorice has been shown to combat bacteria, viruses, yeasts and a wide variety of ailments. **Where found:** disturbed sites, ditches; parkland, prairie.

Golden-bean

Thermopsis rhombifolia

Height: 10–50 cm
Leaves: divided into 3 oval leaflets, each 2–3 cm long, plus 2 lobes (stipules)
Flowers: 1–2 cm long; bright yellow, pea-like, in clusters
Fruit: flattened, curved pods, 3–7 cm

Yellow golden-bean blossoms signal the arrival of spring on the prairies. The Blackfoot called this plant "buffalo-bean" because flowering time coincided with the spring buffalo hunt. • Golden-bean provides bees with pollen and nectar and also attracts native butterflies. Small, brown Afranius duskywing (*Erynnis afranius*) butterflies and their caterpillars use golden-bean as a food source. **Caution:** golden-bean is poisonous and should never be eaten. Eating any part of this plant can lead to severe illness in humans or death in livestock. **Where found:** open, well-drained sites; prairie.

Red Clover

Trifolium pratense

Height: 80 cm
Leaves: 2–5 cm long; 3 leaflets
Flowers: 25–35 mm long; pink to purple, in dense clusters
Fruit: 1-seeded pods

A ubiquitous weedy plant of open ground, red clover has round, pink to purple flowerheads and large leaves. • Native to Europe, clover is widely used around the world as fodder. It depends on bumblebees for pollination, so when clover crops were introduced to Australia, bumblebees were imported, too. Red clovers are heavily used by native butterflies. Clouded sulphurs are fond of nectaring at the blossoms and probably use red clover as a host plant. **Where found:** open, disturbed sites such as roadsides, fields, lawns; throughout.

American Vetch

Vicia americana

Height: 20 cm–1.2 m
Leaves: 15–35 mm long; compound, 8–14 oblong leaflets
Flowers: 15–20 mm long; bluish purple, pea-like
Fruit: pods, 2–3 cm long

Twining tendrils wrap around nearby stems and leaves as this slender vine climbs upward over its neighbours. Its flat, hairless "pea pods" are attractive to young children, but they are not edible. • When an insect lands on a vetch flower, anthers spring out to dust the insect's belly with pollen. The next flower collects the pollen on its stigma and applies another load of pollen. **Where found:** moist, fairly open sites; throughout.

Northern Crane's-bill

Geranium bicknellii

Height: up to 60 cm
Leaves: 2–7 cm wide; roughly 5 sides, deeply cut into 5 toothed segments
Flowers: 1 cm wide; showy, pink-purple, 5 petals
Fruit: long-beaked capsules, up to 2 cm long

This wild geranium species and others in the genus are often called "crane's bill" because of the fruit's resemblance to a crane's head. It is a characteristic spring bloomer of rich woods, often growing in profusion with other wildflowers. This native is an excellent landscaping plant in central and southern areas. • Rubbing a fresh geranium plant, which has a strong smell, on exposed skin and clothes is said to repel mosquitoes. You can try it, but don't discard the bug spray. **Where found:** rich woods; boreal forest, parkland.

Flax

Linum spp.

Height: 30–90 cm
Leaves: 15–35 mm long; lance-shaped
Flowers: 2–3 cm wide; blue, 5 fragile petals
Fruit: round capsules, 6 mm long

The beautiful, delicate, pale to sky blue blossoms of flax usually open in the morning and fade in the hot sun later that day. Most plants produce only one flower at a time, with the next bud opening the following morning. • The stems contain long, tough fibres, similar to those of cultivated flax, which have been used to make ropes, cords, fishing lines and nets. The ground seeds are high in fibre and are a tasty addition to breads or other baked goods. **Where found:** dry, open sites; southern boreal forest, parkland, grasslands.

Spotted Touch-me-not

Impatiens capensis

Height: 50 cm–1.5 m
Leaves: 3–10 cm long; oval, serrate margins
Flowers: 20–25 mm long; orange-yellow, sac-like sepal
Fruit: green capsules, 2 cm long

This plant seems to be made from water. Exceptionally succulent, it practically wilts before your eyes if picked. • The seeds are enclosed in fleshy capsules and held by tightly coiled elastic attachments. Press a ripe pod and the seeds will shoot forth explosively, hence the plant's name. Catch the seeds in your hand, pop 'em in your mouth and enjoy the taste of walnuts. The flowers are irresistible to hummingbirds. • Crushed leaves can treat rashes caused by poison ivy and stinging nettle. **Where found:** moist, shaded woods, damp sites; parkland, boreal forest. **Also known as:** jewelweed.

Leafy Spurge

Euphorbia esula

Height: up to 70 cm
Leaves: 3–8 cm long; elliptic or linear, whorled
Flowers: tiny; greenish, dwarfed by 5 yellow petal-like bracts, in loose cluster
Fruit: 3-lobed capsule, 2 mm wide

Introduced spurge crowds out native plants and greatly reduces rangeland productivity. The prominent yellow "petals" of this species are actually bracts, or appendages, with the tiny true flowers contained in the centre of the bracts. **Caution:** spurge contains a whitish latex that is extremely caustic and irritating, especially in contact with mucous membranes such as in the eyes, nose and mouth. Animal experiments found that the compounds in the latex were 10,000–100,000 times more irritating than capsaicin, the main ingredient in pepper spray. If ingested, it causes nausea, vomiting and diarrhea. **Where found:** disturbed sites, roadsides, cultivated fields; peak abundance on prairie.

Scarlet Globemallow

Sphaeralcea coccinea

Height: 10–20 cm
Leaves: 2–5 cm long; deeply cut into 3–5 narrow lobes
Flowers: 1–2 cm wide; orange to brick red, 5 petals, in clusters
Fruit: many-segmented, hairy discs resembling a cheese wheel

Drought-tolerant scarlet globemallow is a good choice for native wildflower gardens. The segmented fruits look like miniature cheese-rounds, so children sometimes call globemallow fruits "fairy cheeses." • These mucilaginous plants are slimy when crushed. Traditionally, globe-mallow plants were crushed into poultices and used to soothe irritated tissues. **Where found:** dry, open sites; prairie, grasslands.

Canada Violet

Viola canadensis

Height: up to 40 cm
Leaves: 5–10 cm long; broadly heart-shaped
Flowers: 2 cm wide; white with yellow centre and purple veins, 5 petals
Fruit: capsules with tiny dark seeds

Of all our native violets, Canada violet is perhaps the most stately and handsome. You can easily recognize this species by its tall, upright stems and bright white flowers with lemon-yellow centres. Seeds are often dispersed by ants that carry them to their nests then bite off the elaiosome bodies—oily, tasty "ant snacks." • Violet flowers make a pretty garnish for salads, and the cooked or raw leaves are high in vitamins A and C. **Caution:** seeds and rhizomes are poisonous. • Both white and blue-flowered violet species are widespread across our region, including early blue violet (*V. adunca*), found on sandy soils. **Where found:** damp woods; throughout.

Pincushion Cactus

Escobaria vivipara

Height: to 5 cm
Leaves: absent; brownish green spines on 4–5 cm wide, cone-shaped pad (actually stem)
Flowers: 4–5 cm wide; showy, pink to lavender with yellow centre
Fruit: pale green, fleshy berry, brown when mature

Radiant pink to lavender pincushion cactus flowers open in July, but flower buds are produced the previous summer and remain dormant all winter. Watch for them to bloom on open, arid grasslands, especially south-facing slopes in the badlands and up the Qu'Appelle Valley. Birds and small mammals eat the fleshy berries, which are also edible for humans and are said to be delicious. **Where found:** open prairie of southern SK.

Prickly-pear Cactus

Opuntia spp.

Height: prostrate; 5–40 cm tall
Leaves: absent; starburst cluster of spines, to 5 cm long, on 5–7 cm wide pad
Flowers: 4–8 cm wide; bell-shaped, brilliant yellow
Fruit: red-purple, fleshy, spiny, 15–25 mm long

Prickly-pear, though native here, is scattered and local, inhabiting dry, sandy areas—relict habitants of a long ago hotter, drier time. Watch your step! These fleshy cacti are copiously beset with spines. • Prickly-pear were widely used for food by Native peoples. Raw cacti are said to taste like cucumber. Once the spines and seeds were removed, the flesh was eaten raw, used to thicken stews and soups or dried for later use. More recently, the sweet flesh has been added to fruitcakes or canned as fruit juice. Berries can also be boiled whole and strained to make jellies or syrups. **Where found:** rocky outcrops, gravelly soils, sand dunes; scattered sparingly throughout south.

Common Fireweed

Chamerion angustifolium

Height: 3 m (occasionally taller)
Leaves: 2–20 cm long; lance-shaped
Flowers: 1.5–3.5 cm wide; pink to purple, in long, erect clusters
Fruit: narrow, pod-like capsules, 4–8 cm long

Aptly named, fireweed reaches peak abundance immediately after fires and can turn freshly scarred landscapes pink with its blooms. Fireweed serves an important ecological role by stabilizing barren ground, which eventually allows other species of plants to recolonize. The erect, linear pods split lengthwise to release hundreds of tiny seeds tipped with fluffy, white hairs (comas). • Young shoots can be eaten like asparagus, and the flowers can be added to salads. **Where found:** open, often disturbed sites, burned areas; throughout except taiga shield.

Scarlet Beeblossom

Gaura coccinea

Height: 10–40 cm
Leaves: 1–3 cm long; slender, oblong
Flowers: 1 cm wide; scarlet red, cross-shaped, in clusters
Fruit: nut-like capsule, 6 mm long

Once open, scarlet beeblossom flowers begin to change colour. At first, the 4, spoon-shaped petals are white, but they soon take on a pinkish hue. Within a few hours of opening, the whole flower has turned scarlet. • The paired petals of this plant resemble spreading butterfly wings. **Where found:** dry, open sites; parkland, prairies. **Also known as:** butterflyweed.

Common Evening-primrose

Oenothera biennis

Height: 50 cm–1.5 m
Leaves: 10–20 cm long; lance-shaped, slightly toothed
Flowers: 2.5–5 cm long; yellow, tube-shaped, open at dusk
Fruit: cylindrical capsules, 2–3 cm long

The flowers of this well-named species open toward dusk, bloom throughout the night and generally close by mid-morning. Moths are the prime pollinators, so this strategy best accommodates them. Flowers open amazingly quickly, going from shrivelled wisps to robust blossoms in 15–20 minutes. • Evening-primrose is best known for its abundant, oil-rich seeds, which contain essential fatty acids. The seeds are processed into evening-primrose oil, used to treat eczema, high cholesterol, heart disease, PMS, asthma, arthritis and other ailments. The seeds and flowers may be eaten in salads, and young leaves steamed as greens. **Where found:** dry, open sites; southern SK/MB.

Wild Sarsaparilla

Aralia nudicaulis

Height: to 60 cm
Leaves: 3–15 cm long; 3 divisions of 3–5 leaflets, long-stalked
Flowers: 2–5 cm wide; greenish white, in ball-shaped clusters
Fruit: greenish berries turn purple with age, 6 mm long

The roots of this fragrant plant were once widely used to flavour root beer and in medicinal teas. Although the dark purple berries are considered inedible, the root tea was valued as a blood-purifier, tonic and stimulant and was used for treating lethargy, general weakness, stomachaches, fevers and coughs. • Wild sarsaparilla, a member of the ginseng family, is sometimes substituted for true sarsaparilla, (*Smilax* spp.), a member of the lily family. **Where found:** rich, moist woods; parkland, boreal forest.

Spotted Water-hemlock

Cicuta maculata

Height: 60–200 cm
Leaves: 3–10 cm long; compound leaflets
Flowers: small, greenish white, in flat-topped clusters 5–12 cm wide
Fruit: seed-like schizocarps, 2–4 mm wide

Spotted water-hemlock is one of the most poisonous plants in North America. All parts of the plant are poisonous, but most of the toxin is contained in the roots. A single bite can be fatal to humans, who have confused water-hemlock with common water-parsnip (*Sium suave*). Children have been poisoned from using the hollow stems as pea-shooters. Cattle are particularly at risk in early spring, when plants are smaller, more palatable and easily uprooted. • The similar introduced poison-hemlock (*Conium maculatum*) has purple-blotched stems and thinly divided leaves. **Where found:** wet areas; parkland, boreal forest.

Common Cow-parsnip

Heracleum maximum

Height: 1–2.5 m
Leaves: 10–30 cm long; compound, divided into 3 large, toothed leaflets
Flowers: small, in flat-topped clusters 10–20 cm across
Fruit: seed-like schizocarps, 7–12 mm across

The young, fleshy stems of cow-parsnip can be peeled and eaten raw or cooked and are said to taste like celery, but do not confuse cow-parsnip with the deadly poisonous water-hemlocks. Many animals, including bears, eat cow-parsnip. • Toy flutes or whistles can be made from the dry, hollow stems, but they may irritate the lips and cause painful blisters, leading to a medical condition known as "pea-shooter syndrome." **Where found:** moist sites; parkland, boreal forest.

Bunchberry

Cornus canadensis

Height: 5–20 cm
Leaves: 2–8 cm long; deeply veined, in whorl of 4–6
Flowers: tiny; cluster of 5–15, surrounded by 4 white, petal-like bracts
Fruit: round, red drupes (berries), 6–8 mm across

These small flowers are really miniature bouquets of tiny blooms surrounded by showy, white, petal-like bracts. The true flowers, at the centre, are easily overlooked. The large, white bracts attract insects and provide good landing platforms. • The berry-like drupes are edible, raw or cooked. They are not very flavourful, but the crunchy, poppy-like seeds are enjoyable. **Where found:** dry to moist sites; throughout.

Common Pink Wintergreen

Pyrola asarifolia

Height: 10–30 cm
Leaves: 2–6 cm long; rounded, leathery, in basal rosette
Flowers: 8–12 mm across; pink, bell-shaped, nodding
Fruit: rounded capsules, 5–10 mm across

Wintergreens grow in intimate association with soil fungi (mycorrhizae). Some species produce all their food by photosynthesis, but others take their food almost entirely from dead organic matter via mycorrhizae. These fungi are unlikely to be found in a garden environment, so wintergreen plants should not be transplanted. **Where found:** moist, often shady sites; throughout except taiga shield.

Saline Shootingstar

Dodecatheon pulchellum

Height: 5–30 cm
Leaves: 3–20 cm long; basal, oval
Flowers: 15–25 cm across; pinkish purple with yellow collar, 5 upswept petals
Fruit: capsules, 1 mm long

The upswept petals of this flower resemble a shooting star. The band in the centre of the flower can be yellow, orange or reddish purple, and this highly variable species can have hairy or hairless leaves. Thompson Indians called this distinctive flower "beautiful-maiden" and Italians named it "mad-violet." • The rapid vibrations of a bee's wings release the fine, powdery pollen from the downward-facing anthers of this flower. **Where found:** salty flats, moist, open areas; throughout.

Fringed Loosestrife

Lysimachia ciliata

Height: up to 1.2 m
Leaves: 5–12 cm long; opposite, broad, hairy petioles
Flowers: 13–25 mm wide; yellow, 5 pointed corolla lobes
Fruit: small, rounded capsule

Often abundant in summer, fringed loosestrife is named for the prominent fringes of hairs along the leaf petioles. The common name loosestrife is applied to a number of plants, including the invasive, non-native purple loosestrife (*Lythrum salicaria*). • Loosestrife is said to have tranquilizing effects, but scientific support is lacking. **Where found:** moist or wet sites, especially wooded floodplains; southern boreal forest and parkland.

Spreading Dogbane

Apocynum androsaemifolium

Height: 20–70 cm
Leaves: 2–10 cm long; drooping, in pairs
Flowers: 4–12 mm wide; pink, bell-shaped
Fruit: hanging pods (follicles), 5–15 cm long

Traditionally, mature dogbane stems were soaked in water to remove the coarse outer fibres, then rolled against the leg into thread and used for fishing nets, bowstrings and communal rabbit hunting nets. • Butterflies are attracted to the tiny blossoms. The milky white sap is similar to that of milkweeds, which are closely related but in a separate family. Toothed scales on the petals spring inward when touched, catching the mouthparts of unsuspecting, smaller insects. **Caution:** The poisonous, milky sap can cause skin blistering, and ingestion has resulted in sickness and death. **Where found:** well-drained, open sites; southern two-thirds of SK/MB.

Showy Milkweed

Asclepias speciosa

Height: to 2 m
Leaves: 8–15 cm long; opposite, oval, thick, fleshy
Flowers: tiny; pinkish lavender, in rounded clusters 5–7 cm across
Fruit: spiny follicles, in erect clusters

These weedy plants contain glycosides that are toxic to animals and humans, so the insects adapted to feed on them are also toxic and tend to be brightly coloured and conspicuous. Bright colours and bold behaviour in the insect world advertise toxicity; predators quickly learn to avoid them. Monarch butterfly larvae feed solely on milkweed leaves. They absorb the toxic glycosides into their bodies, so both larvae and adult butterflies become poisonous to predators. Several species of milkweed beetles also thrive on milkweed; they are bright orange and black. **Where found:** open sites such as fields, meadows, roadsides; southern SK/MB.

Narrow-leaved Puccoon

Lithospermum incisum

Height: 10–50 cm
Leaves: 1–5 cm long; slender, hairy
Flowers: 1–2 cm across; yellow
Fruit: 4 shiny white nutlets, 3 mm across

Puccoon species have hard, shiny nutlets that were once used as decorative beads. In fact, the scientific name *Lithospermum* stems from the Greek words *lithos* ("stone") and *sperma* ("seed"). • "Puccoon" is an Algonkian word meaning "plants used for dyeing." Boiling the plant roots yields a red dye, which was used in face and body paints and for colouring fabrics. **Where found:** dry, open sites; prairie. **Also known as:** fringed gromwell.

Tall Bluebells

Mertensia paniculata

Height: 30–60 cm
Leaves: 5–15 cm long; elliptic to oblanceolate
Flowers: 25 mm long; pale blue, tubular
Fruit: 4 wrinkled nutlets, 2–5 mm long

One of our most striking displays of early spring wildflowers occurs when masses of bluebells spring from still-cool soil. They explode into dazzling bursts of rich blue blooms, and even the most jaded botanist will pause to admire the show. Look quickly—bluebells are ephemeral, wilting quickly to ugly brown detritus and returning to the soil that spawned them. • The name *Mertensia* honors Franz Karl Mertens, a renowned German botanist. Mertens was primarily a collector of algae. He no doubt appreciated being recognized by this beautiful plant as opposed to only slimy green coatings that inspire "ughs" rather than "oohs." **Where found:** moist or wet woods, bottomlands; throughout.

Blue Giant-hyssop

Agastache foeniculum

Height: 30 cm–1m
Leaves: 2–7 cm long; oval, coarsely toothed, in pairs
Flowers: 6–12 mm long; blue, funnel-shaped in dense 2–10 cm spikes
Fruit: 4 small nutlets

Giant-hyssops make an attractive, useful addition to a wildflower garden. These sun-loving plants are easily propagated from seeds, cuttings or root divisions. The flowerhead can be chewed as a breath-freshener, and the leaves can be used to flavour soups or stews. Leaves may also be brewed into a delicate, anise-flavoured tea, best when brewed weakly. Medicinal teas made from giant-hyssop leaves were traditionally used to treat coughs, colds, chest pains and fevers. **Where found:** deciduous woodlands, well-drained, open sites; parkland, prairie.

Wild Mint

Mentha arvensis

Height: 20–80 cm
Leaves: 2–8 cm long; lance-shaped, paired
Flowers: 4–7 mm long; purplish, whitish or pink, funnel-shaped
Fruit: 4 small, oval nutlets

Delicious, fragrant mint is a well-known, edible plant that can be eaten raw or cooked and is used to flavour salads, stews, meats, sauces, jellies and sweets. Mints make delicious, fragrant teas, cold drinks and even wine. • The active medicinal ingredient, menthol, has been shown to expel gas from and relieve spasms of the digestive tract—hence the advent of the after-dinner mint. Menthol calms smooth muscles (e.g., in the digestive tract), and may relieve coughing and sinus congestion. **Where found:** moist to wet areas, usually near water; throughout except far north.

Wild Bergamot

Monarda fistulosa

Height: up to 1 m
Leaves: 2.5–8 cm long; opposite, lance-shaped
Flowers: 2–3.5 cm long; lavender, 2-lipped, in round clusters 3 cm long
Fruit: tiny; shiny nutlets

Wild bergamot's long, tubular, rose to purplish flowers attract hummingbirds, hawk moths and a large diversity of butterfly species. • This plant provides a spice, potherb and tea (similar to Earl Grey). Dried leaves were burned or sprinkled on items to repel insects—rather ironic considering that the living flowers are insect magnets. • This showy, aromatic perennial can easily be grown from seed in gardens, thus bringing a butterfly parade to your yard. **Where found:** old fields, woodland edges, open sites; parkland, prairie.

Common Red Paintbrush

Castilleja miniata

Height: 20–60 cm
Leaves: 5–7 cm; lance-shaped, 3-lobed tip
Flowers: 2–3 cm long; tubular, hidden by showy scarlet bracts
Fruit: capsules, 9–12 mm long

It is usually easy to recognize a paintbrush but difficult to say which of the 150–200 species you have. *Castilleja* is a confusing genus, with many flower shapes and colours, and its species often hybridize. Paintbrushes join roots with nearby plants to steal nutrients, and many depend on their neighbours for sustenance. Showy, red bracts give these flower clusters their colour. The tubular flowers are greenish with a short, broad lower lip and a long, slender upper lip over half as long as the tube. **Where found:** open, well-drained sites; throughout southern boreal forest, parkland, prairie.

Butter-and-eggs

Linaria vulgaris

Height: 30–80 cm
Leaves: 2–6 cm long; slender
Flowers: 20–35 mm; yellow with orange lip, snapdragon-like
Fruit: rounded capsules, 8–12 mm long

Butter-and-eggs is a native of Eurasia that spreads rapidly by both hardy, creeping roots and plentiful seeds (up to 8700 per plant). Cut flowers are quite resilient and last long in the vase. • Most animals avoid this pungent and potentially toxic plant, but large pollinating insects appreciate its abundant flowers. To access nectar, insects must be strong enough to pry apart the snapdragon-like flowers. **Where found:** disturbed sites; parkland, prairie. **Also known as:** toadflax.

False-toadflax

Comandra umbellata

Height: 10–30 cm
Leaves: 1–3 cm long; slender
Flowers: 3–5 mm across; white to pinkish, in oval clusters
Fruit: brownish drupes, 4–8 mm long

Pretty white flowers disguise this plant's sinister side. False-toadflax is a parasitic plant that steals water and nutrients from the roots of neighbouring plants. By extending spreading underground stems and attaching sucker-like organs to nearby roots, false-toadflax supplements its nutrient intake. **Where found:** moist woods, open areas with gravel; parkland, boreal forest.

Northern Bedstraw

Galium boreale

Height: 20–60 cm
Leaves: 2–6 cm long; narrow, in whorls of 4
Flowers: 4–7 mm across; white, in clusters
Fruit: paired nutlets, < 1.5–2 mm across

Bedstraws are related to coffee, and their tiny, paired, short-hairy nutlets can be dried, roasted and ground as a coffee substitute. • Bedstraw juice or tea was once applied to many skin problems. Today, some people take the tea to speed weight loss, but continual use irritates the mouth, and people with poor circulation or diabetes should not use it. • The flowers are arranged in repeatedly 3-forked clusters. • Sweet-scented bedstraw (*G. triflorum*) has whorls of 6 broader, bristle-tipped leaves, and its nutlets are covered with long, hooked bristles. **Where found:** open sites; throughout.

Bluets

Houstonia caerulea

Height: up to 15 cm
Leaves: up to 12 mm long; mostly basal or opposite, spatulate
Flowers: 12 mm wide; whitish blue with yellow centre, tubular, 4-lobed
Fruit: capsules, <7 mm long

Bluets grow en masse and often mist the ground with carpets of blue in spring. They cannot withstand much competition from other plants, and typically grow in barren soil. • The tiny flowers' bright yellow centre acts like a runway for insects, guiding tiny bees to the pollen found inside the tubular flower. The flowers also attract the bumblebee-like beefly, a small hovering insect. **Where found:** dry, barren soil of deciduous forests, clearings; throughout but increasingly scarce northward.

Harebell

Campanula rotundifolia

Height: 10–50 cm
Leaves: 1–6 cm long; narrow stem leaves, rounded basal leaves
Flowers: 2 cm long; purple-blue, bell shaped
Fruit: capsules, 5–8 mm long

From open woodlands to exposed, rocky slopes, these delicate, nodding bells bob in the breeze on thin, wiry stems. • The small openings at the base of the capsules close quickly in damp weather, protecting the seeds from excess moisture. On dry, windy days, the capsules swing widely in the breeze, scattering the seeds. • The species name *rotundifolia* refers to this plant's round, basal leaves. **Where found:** moist to dry, open sites; throughout.

Common Yarrow

Achillea millefolium

Height: 30–90 cm
Leaves: 5–15 cm long; feathery appearance
Flowers: <7 mm long; white, in flat-topped cluster
Fruit: compressed achenes

The fern-like leaves of this member of the sunflower family (Asteraceae) are distinctive. Yarrow is often weedy, and both native and introduced populations occur in our region. • This hardy, aromatic perennial has served for thousands of years as a fumigant, insecticide and medicine. The Greek hero Achilles, for whom the genus was named, used it to help heal his soldiers' wounds. • The flowerheads are white (sometimes pinkish) and the seed-like fruits are hairless and flattened. • Yarrow is an attractive ornamental, but beware—its extensive underground stems (rhizomes) soon invade your garden. **Where found:** dry to moist, open sites; throughout.

Pussytoes

Antennaria spp.

Height: to 25 cm
Leaves: 1–5 cm long; mainly basal, slender, woolly grey
Flowers: cluster of white disc flowers above woolly bracts
Fruit: seed-like achenes

Downy flower clusters of this plant resemble the toes of a kitten. As the flowers dry, the down-tipped seeds parachute away on the wind. • Pussytoes are widespread across our region, and there are several different species of these hardy perennials. They have a pleasant fragrance and keep their shape and colour when dried—excellent for dried flower arrangements. **Where found:** roadsides, fields, open sites; throughout.

Common Burdock

Arctium minus

Height: to 1.5 m
Leaves: to 50 cm long; oval to heart-shaped; woolly underside
Flowers: 15–20 mm; bur-like, spherical cluster of purplish florets
Fruit: seed-like achenes

The hooked bristles of these bur-like flowerheads are said to have inspired the invention of Velcro. • These large, vitamin- and iron-rich plants were originally brought to North America as food plants. All parts of the plants are edible but should not be consumed by pregnant women or diabetics. Young leaves have been used in salads or boiled as a potherb, and roots can be mashed into patties and fried. Some First Nations dried burdock roots for winter supplies or roasted and ground them for use as a coffee substitute. **Where found:** disturbed sites; parkland, prairie.

Nodding Beggar's-ticks

Bidens cernua

Height: up to 1 m (depauperate plants often only a few cm tall)
Leaves: 4–16 cm long; opposite, lance-shaped, sessile or bases fused together around stem
Flowers: 1 cm long; 6–8 yellow ray flowers
Fruit: achenes, 5–7 mm long, with 2–4 barbed bristles

Both the common name beggar's-ticks and the species name *Bidens* (from *bis* ["two"] and *dens* ["teeth" or "prongs"]), refer to the flattened, 2-barbed fruits that easily attach to clothing and animals but are difficult to brush off. "Nodding" refers to the large, marigold-like, drooping flowerheads. • This plant is extremely variable in stature, depending on where it grows. On sun-baked mudflats, it might be a few centimetres tall; on lush ground it may reach 1 m or more. **Where found:** damp soils near water; southern boreal forest, parkland.

Canada Thistle

Cirsium arvense

Height: 30 cm–1.5 m
Leaves: 5–15 cm long; spiny-toothed
Flowers: pink-purple disc flowers, in heads 15–25 mm across
Fruit: seed-like achenes

Canada thistle was introduced to Canada from Europe in the 17th century, then expanded its range into the United States, where it acquired its common name. Today this aggressive weed is found in virtually all croplands and pastures. Prickly thistle colonies choke out other plants and reduce crop yields. Colonies grow from deep underground runners that contain tricin, a substance that inhibits the growth of nearby plants. Each year, one plant can send out up to 6 m of runners, and female plants can release up to 40,000 seeds. • These plants can be beneficial: flowers provide a good source of pollen and nectar for honeybees, and humans can eat the shoots and roots. **Where found:** disturbed sites; southern boreal forest, parkland.

Great Blanketflower

Gaillardia aristata

Height: 20–70 cm
Leaves: 5–15 cm long; lance-shaped
Flowers: 3–7 cm across; yellow with purplish centre
Fruit: 3-sided achenes with papery, 1 cm long

The flamboyant flowers of blanketflower might be mistaken for garden escapees, and in fact many cultivars have been developed from this beautiful native wildflower. It is hardy and easily grown from seed. • Tea from the roots was taken to relieve stomach and intestinal inflammation, reduce hair loss and soothe sore eyes. • This perennial has hairy leaves and stems, and the seed-like fruits are densely hairy, tipped with 6–10 stiff, white bristles. **Where found:** dry, fairly open sites; prairie.

Curly-cup Gumweed

Grindelia squarrosa

Height: 20–60 cm
Leaves: 1–4 cm long; oblong, clasp stem
Flowers: 2–3 cm across; yellow florets around sticky, backward-curving green bracts
Fruit: seed-like achenes, with slender bristles

These bushy, aromatic herbs are common on dry roadsides in late summer. The tough plants are drought resistant. • The resin-dotted leaves and flat-topped clusters of sticky flowerheads have sedative, antispasmodic and expectorant qualities, and they have been used for many years to treat coughing, congestion, asthma and bronchitis. Each seed-like fruit has 4–5 ribs. **Where found:** dry, open sites; prairie.

Common Sunflower

Helianthus annus

Height: to 3 m
Leaves: 6–25 cm long; oval to heart-shaped
Flowers: 5–15 cm across; yellow with red-brown centre
Fruit: seed-like achenes (sunflower seeds), up to 1 cm long

Common sunflower is one of the very few plants cultivated by First
Nations peoples. Some sunflower seeds were eaten raw, but most were
dried, parched, ground lightly to break their shells, and poured into
a container of water, where the kernels sank and the shells floated.
The shells were skimmed off, roasted and used to make a coffee-like
beverage. The kernels were eaten whole or ground into meal for gruel
or light-weight, high-energy cakes. Oil from the seeds was also used in
candle and soap making. The flowers provided a superior yellow dye, and the seeds
were made into black or purple dyes. **Where found:** moist, disturbed sites; grasslands.

Narrow-leaved Hawkweed

Hieracium umbellatum

Height: to 1 m
Leaves: 1–8 cm long; lance-shaped
Flowers: 25 mm across; yellow head, in flat-topped cluster
Fruit: seed-like achenes, 2–3 mm long

Loose clusters of miniature, dandelion-like flowers on long, slender stems
mark this common wildflower. The showy flowerheads attract insects,
but fertilization is rare. Most offspring are genetically identical to the
parent plant. The fruits are cylindrical achenes with tufts of tawny
hairs. • Hawkweed's milky sap contains a rubbery latex, and
Native peoples chewed the leaves of these plants like gum. **Where
found:** moist to wet, open sites; throughout except taiga shield.

Common Blue Lettuce

Lactuca tatarica

Height: to 1 m
Leaves: 5–12 cm long; narrow, lance-shaped (grass-like)
Flowers: 25 mm across; blue to purplish ray flowers
Fruit: thin achenes, 4–7 mm long

Blue lettuce and other *Lactuca* species may cause skin irritation or
internal poisoning. When collected and dried, the milky sap forms the
drug known as lactucarium, also called lettuce opium because of its
sedative and analgesic properties. Used as far back as ancient Egypt,
lettuce opium was viewed as a weak alternative to opium that did not
have the side effects of addiction and intestinal upset. In 1898, it was
introduced and standardized as a drug in the U.S. for use in lozenges, tinctures and
syrups as a sedative, for dry cough, whooping cough, insomnia, anxiety and other
ailments. **Where found:** woods, clearings; parkland, prairie.

Oxeye Daisy

Leucanthemum vulgare

Height: 20–90 cm
Leaves: 4–15 cm long; deeply lobed, becoming smaller up the stem
Flowers: heads 2.5–5 cm across; 15–35 white ray flowers surround yellow disc flowers
Fruit: seed-like achenes

A favourite among children, daisies can be braided into necklaces and crowns or plucked apart to the verse "He loves me, he loves me not." • Bright, white and yellow oxeye daisies were introduced from Eurasia 400 years ago and now carpet fields, ditches and abandoned lots across North America. Despite being a common weed that competes against native plants and crops, daisies are often depicted as cheerful, welcome additions to gardens. • The shasta daisy (*Chrysanthemum maximum*) is a larger, more robust ornamental variety. **Where found:** open, disturbed areas; southern boreal forest, parkland.

Dotted Blazingstar

Liatris punctata

Height: 10–60 cm
Leaves: 3–15 cm long; slender, stiff, with many dots
Flowers: 10–15 mm across; purple to rose, 4–6 tubular florets in dense spike
Fruit: seed-like achenes with feathery bristles, 7 mm long

This native wildflower makes an excellent addition to prairie gardens. The colourful, long-lasting flower spikes attract bees and make outstanding cut flowers. Plants are easily grown from seed, prefer full sun and are anchored by a thick taproot that can reach 4.5 m deep. • Blazingstar looks similar to and is a safe replacement for purple loosestrife (*Lythrum salacaria*), an introduced, invasive flower known for choking out wetland species. **Where found:** dry, open sites; prairies.

Pineapple-weed

Matricaria discoidea

Height: 5–40 cm
Leaves: 1–5 cm long; pinnately divided 2–3 times, thread-like
Flowers: 5–9 mm across; yellow, cone-shaped
Fruit: seed-like achenes

Pineapple-weed is a close relative of wild chamomile (*M. recutita*) and gives off a similar, pineapple-like aroma when crushed. This aromatic plant can be used as an air freshener, insect repellent or deodorizing hand wash after handling fish. The young flowerheads can be steeped into a soothing tea or eaten raw in salads. • Like closely related ragweed (*Ambrosia* spp.), pineapple-weed can cause allergic reaction in some people. • Look for this common weed growing along sidewalks, roadsides or in other areas with poor, compacted soil. **Where found:** open, disturbed sites; southern boreal forest, parkland, grasslands.

Coltsfoot

Petasites frigidus

Height: 10–50 cm
Leaves: 10–30 cm long; basal; variable arrow-shaped, rounded or deeply lobed
Flowers: 8 mm across; whitish, in dense, rounded cluster
Fruit: seed-like achene with silky hairs in fluffy white heads

The coltsfoots, though very different in appearance because of their distinctive leaf shapes, are now considered varieties of one species, *P. frigidus*. • Coltsfoot is said to be soothing because it contains mucilage and compounds with antispasmodic and sedative effects. Dried coltsfoot has been used for hundreds of years to make medicinal teas to relieve coughing and pain from chest colds, whooping cough, asthma and viral pneumonia. It is also reported to contain antihistamines. Pregnant women should not eat this plant. **Where found:** moist to wet areas; parkland, boreal forest and northward.

Prairie Coneflower

Ratibida columnifera

Height: 30–70 cm
Leaves: to 10 cm long; pinnately divided into 5–9 lobes
Flowers: hanging, yellow florets surround 1–4 cm long, yellow to brown cone
Fruit: tiny, dark grey, seed-like achenes

The flowers of this plant look like small hats—a ring of yellow florets form a brim around a tall, cylindrical brown crown. These distinctive, native wildflowers are hardy choices for dry prairie gardens and are popular in restoration work. • Once dried, the edible cones are said to taste like corn but can be chewy and are best picked when young. An enjoyable tea can be brewed from the leaves. **Where found:** dry, open, disturbed sites; prairie.

Black-eyed Susan

Rudbeckia hirta

Height: up to 1 m
Leaves: 5–17 cm long; narrow, oblong
Flowers: 5–10 cm across; 10–20 yellow-orange florets surround brown disc
Fruit: brown, seed-like achenes

In the past century, this native flower of the American Midwest has spread across North America. The gorgeous yellow-orange blossoms adorn many gardens and make excellent, long-lasting cut flowers. Dried or pressed flowers retain their cheery colour. • Medicinally, the plant was taken internally to increase urination or expel worms. It was also used in a wash to soothe snakebites and wounds. **Where found:** open, disturbed sites; parkland, prairie.

Marsh Ragwort

Senecio congestus

Height: 20 cm–1 m
Leaves: 5–15 cm long; wavy edges
Flowers: 1–2 cm across; yellow, in flat-topped cluster
Fruit: seed-like achenes, tipped with fluffy white hairs

These hairy plants form yellow rings around prairie ponds. In undisturbed sites, ragwort often occurs singly or in small numbers. • Allergy sufferers beware: this plant produces huge amounts of allergenic pollen. The species name *congestus* refers to the cluster of flowerheads, though, not to congested noses! *Senicio* comes from the Latin *senex,* or old man, referring to the fuzzy seedheads. **Where found:** moist sites, disturbed areas; boreal forest, parkland. **Also known as:** woolly-mammoth plant.

Canada Goldenrod

Solidago canadensis

Height: 30 cm–1.2 m
Leaves: 5–10 cm long; lance-shaped
Flowers: tiny; ray and disc flowers, in pyramidal clusters
Fruit: small, hairy seed-like achenes

Many people blame these bold, pyramid-shaped flower clusters for causing allergies, but the real culprit is probably a less conspicuous plant, such as ragweed (*Ambrosia* spp.), which shares the same habitat. Goldenrod pollen is too heavy to be carried by the wind; instead, it is carried by flying insects. • Each seed-like fruit is tipped with parachutes of white hairs. **Where found:** moist, open fields, woods, roadsides; throughout.

Perennial Sow-thistle

Sonchus arvensis

Height: 40 cm–2 m
Leaves: 5–40 cm long; deeply lobed, prickly edges
Flowers: heads 3–5 cm across; yellow ray flowers
Fruit: achenes, 2.5–3.5 mm across

Tall perennial sow-thistle is something like a dandelion on steroids, growing taller and faster than neighbouring plants. Hardy roots and abundant seeds help it spread rapidly, outcompeting crops for moisture, nutrients and sunlight. • The young leaves taste similar to lettuce and may be used in salads, along with the edible flowerheads. Older leaves can be cooked as a vegetable. • This plant is devoured by livestock and rabbits and is a host plant for aphids. **Where found:** disturbed sites; parkland, prairie.

Fringed Aster

Symphyotrichum ciliolatum

Height: 20 cm–1.2 m
Leaves: 4–12 cm long
Flowers: heads 15–30 mm across; purple-blue ray flowers surround yellow disc
Fruit: seed-like achenes, with parachute of silky hairs

These cheerful, purplish asters beautify many of our trails, clearings and roadsides. The aster family contains many different species, but fringed aster's large, heart-shaped lower leaves make it easy to identify. • Traditionally, the roots of this plant were boiled to treat pink eye or crushed and applied as a poultice to stop bleeding. • The name aster means "star" and refers to the shape of the flowers. **Where found:** open, disturbed areas, forests; throughout.

Common Tansy

Tanacetum vulgare

Height: 40 cm–1 m
Leaves: 10–20 cm long; fern-like, hairy, gland-dotted
Flowers: 1 cm across; yellow disc flowers, in dense, button-like heads
Fruit: tiny; seed-like achenes

Yellow, button-like flowers top common tansy, a medicinal and horticultural herb introduced from Europe. This rapidly spreading weed is often found in ditches or along rivers, where the current carries the seeds downstream. • **Caution:** Tansy contains toxic volatile oils that are potentially fatal, and plants have been strewn on floors to repel insects and boiled into an insecticide or a wash for lice or scabies. **Where found:** disturbed sites; southern boreal forest, parkland.

Common Dandelion

Taraxacum officinale

Height: 5–50 cm
Leaves: 5–40 cm long; basal, deeply lobed
Flowers: 2–5 cm wide; numerous yellow rays, disc flowers absent
Fruit: tiny; achenes in white, fluffy pappus

Dandelions must be the most widely recognized forb in our range. Emerald green lawns sprinkled with yellow blossoms create a rather showy palette but rankle fastidious lawn-keepers. • These vitamin-rich greens have been receiving positive press lately. Brought to North America from Eurasia, they were cultivated for food and medicine. Young dandelion leaves and flowerheads are chock full of vitamins and minerals and make nutritious additions to salads. They can be cooked like vegetables, added to pancakes, muffins or fritters, or even made into wine. The roots can be ground into a caffeine-free coffee substitute or boiled to make a red dye. **Where found:** disturbed sites; throughout.

Common Goat's-beard

Tragopogon dubius

Height: 30–100 cm
Leaves: 5–50 cm long; grass-like, base clasps stem
Flowers: 25–65 mm across; yellow florets and long, pointed green bracts
Fruit: seed-like achenes with feathery, parachute-like hair

Yellow goat's-beard flowers may be overlooked, but the gigantic, dandelion-like seedheads are hard to miss. Each seed is attached to a downy parachute that floats on the wind, carrying it great distances. • Thick, fleshy goat's-beard roots can be eaten raw, roasted or boiled and are said to taste like parsnips. Dried, roasted roots have also been used as a coffee substitute. **Where found:** open, disturbed sites; boreal plain, parkland, prairie.

Ostrich Fern

Matteuccia struthiopteris

Height: 50 cm–1.5 m
Leaves: 50 cm–1.5 m long; sterile fronds, plume-like
Spore clusters: on shorter, fertile fronds 20–60 cm long

Fiddleheads, the coiled fronds of the young ferns, are an excellent wild edible that is sold commercially. The large fiddleheads taste a bit like asparagus and are rich in vitamins A and C. When harvesting, no more than 3 tops per plant should be taken, because over-picking depletes the rhizome's energy reserves and kills the plant. • Fiddleheads are so named because of their resemblance to the scroll of a violin. **Where found:** wet to moist forests, wetlands, riparian areas, roadsides; boreal forest.

Common Horsetail

Equisetum arvense

Height: up to 50 cm tall
Leaves: small scales
Spore clusters: blue-tipped cones

Next time you come across a horsetail, feel the stem. Silica crystals cause the rough texture and strengthen the plant. First Nations peoples used the abrasive horsetails like sandpaper to smooth tools. • Most people are familiar with this plant's sterile "horse tail" stems that have many whorls of slender branches, but common horsetail also sprouts unbranched, fertile stems that are often overlooked. These smaller, brownish shoots have blunt cones at their tips and look similar to slender mushrooms. **Where found:** moist to wet forests, wetlands, disturbed sites; throughout except taiga shield.

Buck-bean

Menyanthes trifoliata

Height: 10–30 cm
Leaves: 3–8 cm long; long-stalked, divided into 3 leaflets
Flowers: 2 cm across; white, 5 hairy, spreading petals, in clusters
Fruit: 6–9 mm long; oval capsules

Three leaflets growing on a long stalk mark this plant. The foliage looks similar to broad-bean leaves, which may be where the "bean" part of the name comes from. • This bitter plant has few traditional uses. Europeans sometimes substituted buck-bean leaves for hops in beer making or mixed the dried, powdered roots with flour in times of famine. **Where found:** standing water; throughout except extreme north and southwest.

Arum-leaved Arrowhead

Sagittaria cuneata

Height: 20–50 cm
Leaves: 6–12 cm long; arrowhead-shaped
Flowers: to 1 cm long; white, showy, 3 petals, in clusters of 3
Fruit: beaked achenes in clustered heads

This beautiful, characteristic plant of marshes can be extremely variable in leaf shape, though it always has long basal lobes. Arrowhead flowers are some of the showiest in a marsh—small whorls of white, 3-parted blossoms. • The entire rootstock is edible, but the corms are preferred. When cooked, corms taste like potatoes or chestnuts, but they are unpleasant raw. Waterfowl also eagerly root out and eat the corms. **Where found:** shallow water or mud of sunny marshes, ditches, other wetlands; parkland and boreal forest.

Thread-leaved Watercrowfoot

Ranunculus trichophyllus

Height: mat-forming, floating perennial
Leaves: repeatedly divided into 3s, in hair-like segments
Flowers: 10–15 mm across; white, saucer-shaped, 5 petals
Fruit: oval, seed-like achenes, 2 mm long

Watercrowfoot belongs to the buttercup family and can only survive in water. Clumps or floating mats of this thread-leaved plant provide hiding places for water bugs, shrimp and tadpoles. A variety of different species are found across our region, with either white or yellow flowers. • The name crowfoot comes from the leaf's resemblance to the foot of a crow. **Where found:** still, shallow water; parkland, boreal forest and north past treeline.

Yellow Pond-lily

Nuphar lutea

Height: floating aquatic perennial
Leaves: 7–35 cm long; heart-shaped floating
Flowers: 35–60 mm across; yellow
Fruit: spongy berries, 20–45 mm across

This floating, aquatic perennial grows from a large, buried rootstock. Some Native groups sliced the rootstocks and then ate them fried or boiled, or dried and ground them into flour, but other groups considered them inedible. If eaten in large amounts, pond-lily rootstocks can be poisonous. Dried, sliced rootstocks were made into medicinal teas and used to treat arthritis, headaches, sore throats and heart problems or to aid in childbirth. **Where found:** still waters; boreal forest, occasionally northern parkland.

Water Calla

Calla palustris

Height: 10–30 cm; aquatic perennial from rootstock
Leaves: 5–10 cm long; oval to heart-shaped, on long stalks
Flowers: showy white bract, 2–7 cm long, surrounds pale yellow spadix
Fruit: red, berry-like, in cluster

These beautiful plants have a fiery side—all parts contain calcium oxalate crystals that inflame soft tissues and cause a strong burning sensation in the mouth and digestive tract. Animals tend to leave this plant alone. • The name calla comes from *kallos,* the Greek word for "beautiful." **Where found:** still, shallow waters; throughout except taiga shield and southwestern SK. **Also known as:** water-dragon.

Water Smartweed

Polygonum amphibium

Height: terrestrial form up to 90 cm
Leaves: 2–15 cm long; lance-shaped, pointed, often reddish
Flowers: <6 cm wide; in dense, spike-like clusters
Fruit: dark achenes, 3 mm long

This species is easily the showiest of our many native smartweeds, sending forth large, flaming pink spikes of flowers. There are 2 forms: variety *stipulaceum* grows in deep water and has floating leaves; variety *emersum* grows in moist soil and is stiffer and more upright. • Smartweed achenes are a winter staple for birds, including ducks, rails, geese, sparrows and redpolls. Chipmunks, squirrels, small rodents and deer eat the plants and fruit. The edible leaves have a hot, peppery taste and are very high in vitamins K and C. They can be used fresh in salads or eaten as a steamed vegetable. • The achenes can remain dormant in soil for decades, germinating when conditions become suitable. **Where found:** shallow ponds, lakes, streams, wetlands; throughout.

Common Bladderwort

Utricularia vulgaris

Height: floating aquatic perennial
Leaves: minute; submerged or floating, linear with tiny bladder
Flowers: 1 cm long; yellow, 2-lipped corolla
Fruit: tiny capsules

Like tiny yellow violets, the flowers of this bizarre aquatic meat-eater jut from the water's surface. Most carnivorous plants trap and eat insects, but aquatic bladderworts digest everything from tiny worms to small crustaceans. Like other carnivorous plants, bladderworts are typically found in cold, acidic, nitrogen-poor environments. These plants get their nitrogen from the invertebrates they digest, so they are able to grow where others cannot survive. • Other bladderworts are found in our region, but common bladderwort is easily the most frequent species. It floats in water or creeps along muddy shores, its tiny bladders festooning roots and providing the "traps" to capture prey. **Where found:** shallow to deep waters of ponds, lakes, marshes; throughout.

Common Cattail

Typha latifolia

Height: up to 3 m
Leaves: up to 3 m long, up to 2 cm wide; linear
Flowers: tiny; yellowish green, in dense spikes 8–14 cm long
Fruit: achenes in fuzzy brown spike (cattail), 10–20 cm long

Cattails rim wetlands and line lakeshores and ditches across North America, providing cover for many animals. They are critical for supporting least bitterns, marsh wrens and other marsh birds. • Cattails grow from long rhizomes that were traditionally eaten fresh in spring. Later in the season, when the rhizomes became bitter with maturity, they were peeled and roasted or dried and ground into flour. • Fresh, dried seedheads were used to bandage burns and promote healing. **Where found:** marshes, ponds, ditches, damp ground; throughout.

Big Bluestem

Andropogon gerardii

Height: 1–2.5 m
Leaves: 10–5 cm long; blue-green, flat to V-shaped
Flowers: 5–10 cm long; 3–6 purplish racemes with fine hairs

Big bluestem is also known as "turkey foot" because the flower clusters often branch out in groups of 3. This signature grass of the tall-grass prairie once stretched across southern Manitoba and southeastern Saskatchewan but now remains only in small, protected patches. In dry conditions, the leaves of bluestem roll up to conserve water. Big bluestem is an excellent forage plant for livestock and a superior choice for landscapers seeking a native, drought-tolerant grass. **Where found:** moist to dry conditions; tall-grass prairie.

Blue Grama Grass

Bouteloua gracilis

Height: 20–50 cm
Leaves: 2–15 cm long; flat, curled, rough, tapered at tip
Flowers: 1.5–4 cm long; bluish purple, curved like eyelashes

A common grass of the short-grass prairie, blue grama has young flowerheads that look like tiny combs and later resemble false eyelashes. The dense, shallow roots of this grass quickly absorb water, hold down the soil and prevent wind erosion. Blue grama is valued for landscaping, reclamation work and as forage. • Blackfoot peoples used the spiky fruiting stems to predict winter weather. One fruiting branch per stem indicated a mild winter, and 3 or more meant a tough winter ahead. **Where found:** sandy soils; prairie.

Needle-and-thread Grass

Hesperostipa comata

Height: 30–70 cm
Leaves: 10–30 cm long; wide, flat, rolled in
Flowers: pointed seed fruits and long, curled, thread-like awns

Needle-and-thread grass is named for its thread-like awns and slender, pointed, needle-like seed fruits. The hygroscopic awns wind and unwind with changes in temperature and moisture, drilling the pointed seeds into the soil to increase their chances of germinating. Bunches grow from a deep root system. • Needle-and-thread grass, a dominant grass of mixed grasslands and also common in parkland, was selected as Saskatchewan's provincial grass emblem in 2001. **Where found:** sandy soils; parkland, prairie.

Foxtail Barley

Hordeum jubatum

Height: 30–60 cm
Leaves: 5–15 cm long; flat, bluish green
Flowers: 5–10 cm long; graceful, nodding spikes, yellow to bronze

Fuzzy foxtail barley is a native perennial that grows in bunches from shallow roots. It prefers, moist, fertile soils but will thrive under extreme environmental conditions such as drought, flooding or salinity. The barbed awns are carried away by the wind, catch onto clothing or hook onto passing animals then work their way inward. The awns can cause serious injury if lodged in the eyes, nose or mouth of dogs or livestock. **Where found:** disturbed sites including sloughs, roadsides, stream edges; throughout.

GLOSSARY

A

achene: a seed-like fruit, e.g., sunflower seed

algae: simple photosynthetic aquatic plants lacking true stems, roots, leaves and flowers, and ranging in size from single-celled forms to giant kelp

altricial: animals that are helpless at birth or hatching

anadromous: fish that migrate from salt water to fresh water to spawn

annual: plants that live for only 1 year or growing season

anterior: situated at or toward the front

aquatic: water frequenting

arboreal: tree frequenting

arthropod: joint-limbed organisms with hard exoskeletons; from the phylum Arthropoda, which includes crustaceans, centipedes, insects and spiders

autotrophic: an organism that produces its own food, e.g., by photosynthesis

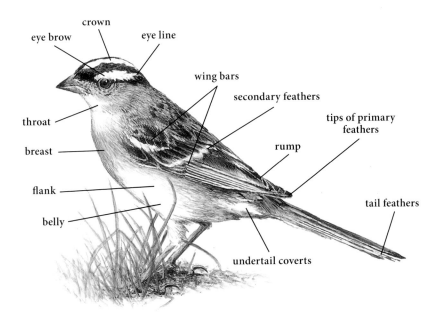

B

barbels: fleshy, whisker-like appendages found on some fish

basal leaf: a leaf arising from the base of a plant

benthic: bottom feeding

berry: a fleshy fruit, usually with several to many seeds

bract: a leaf-like structure arising from the base of a flower or inflorescence

bracteole: a small bract borne on a leaf stalk

brood parasite: a bird that parasitizes other bird's nests by laying its eggs and then abandoning them for the parasitized birds to raise, e.g., brown-headed cowbird

bulb: a fleshy underground organ with overlapping, swollen scales, e.g., an onion

C

calyx: a collective term for the sepals of a flower

cambium: inner layers of tissue that transport nutrients up and down the plant stalk or trunk

canopy: the fairly continuous cover provided by the branches and leaves of adjacent trees

capsules: a dry fruit that splits open to release seeds

carapace: a protective bony shell (e.g., of a turtle) or exoskeleton (e.g., of beetles)

carnivorous: feeding primarily on meat

carrion: decomposing animal matter or carcass

catkin: a spike of small flowers

chelipeds: the clawed first pair of legs, e.g., on a crab

compound leaf: a leaf separated into 2 or more divisions called leaflets

cone: the fruit produced by a coniferous plant, composed of overlapping scales round a central axis

coniferous: cone-bearing; seed (female) and pollen (male) cones are borne on the same tree in different locations

corm: a swollen underground stem base used by some plants as an organ of propagation; resembles a bulb

crepuscular: active primarily at dusk and dawn

cryptic coloration: a coloration pattern designed to conceal an animal

D

deciduous: a tree whose leaves turn color and are shed annually

defoliating: dropping of the leaves

disk flower: a small flower in the centre, or disk, of a composite flower (e.g., aster, daisy or sunflower)

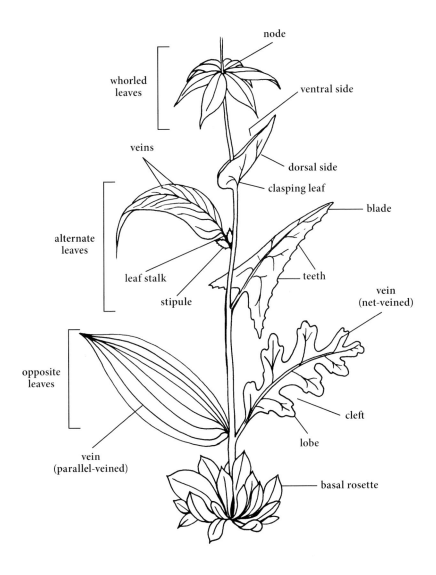

diurnal: active primarily during the day

dorsal: the top or back

drupe: a fleshy fruit with a stony pit, e.g., peach, cherry

E

echolocation: navigation by rebounding sound waves off objects to target or avoid them

ecological niche: an ecological role filled by a species

ecoregion: distinction between regions based upon geology, climate, biodiversity, elevation and soil composition

ectoparasites: skin parasites

ectotherm: an animal that regulates its body temperature behaviourally from external sources of heat, i.e., from the sun

eft: the stage of a newt's life following the tadpole stage, in which it exits the water and leads a terrestrial life; when the newt matures to adulthood it returns to the water

endemic: a species with a distribution that is geographically restricted to a limited area or region

endotherm: an animal that regulates its body temperature internally

estivate: a state of inactivity and a slowing of the metabolism to permit survival in extended periods of high temperatures and inadequate water supply

estuarine: an area where a freshwater river exits into the sea; the salinity of the seawater drops because it is diluted by the fresh water

eutrophic: a nutrient-rich body of water with an abundance of algae growth and a low level of dissolved oxygen

evergreen: having green leaves through winter; not deciduous

exoskeleton: a hard outer encasement that provides protection and points of attachment for muscles

F

flight membrane: the membrane between the fore and hind limbs of bats and some squirrels that allows bats to fly and squirrels to glide through the air

follicle: the structure in the skin from which hair or feathers grow; a dry fruit that splits open along a single line on one side when ripe; a cocoon

food web: the elaborated, interconnected feeding relationships of living organisms in an ecosystem

forb: a broad-leaved plant that lacks a permanent woody stem and loses its aboveground growth each year; may be annual, biennial or perennial

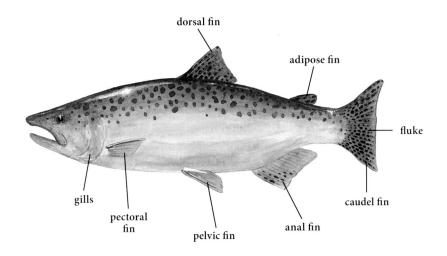

dorsal fin

adipose fin

fluke

gills

pectoral fin

pelvic fin

anal fin

caudel fin

G

gillrakers: long, thin, fleshy projections that protect delicate gill tissue from particles in the water

glandular: similar to or containing glands

H

habitat: the physical area in which an organism lives

hawking: feeding behaviour in which a bird leaves a perch, snatches its prey in mid-air, and then returns to its previous perch

herbaceous: feeding primarily on vegetation

hibernation: a state of decreased metabolism and body temperature and slowed heart and respiratory rates to permit survival during long periods of cold temperature and diminished food supply

hibernaculum: a shelter in which an animal, usually a mammal, reptile or insect, chooses to hibernate

hips: the berry-like fruit of some plants in the rose family (Rosaceae)

hybrids: the offspring from a cross between parents belonging to different varieties or subspecies, sometimes between different subspecies or genera

I

incubate: to keep eggs at a relatively constant temperature until they hatch

inflorescence: a cluster of flowers on a stalk; may be arranged as a spike, raceme, head, panicle, etc.

insectivorous: feeding primarily on insects

invertebrate: any animal lacking a backbone, e.g., worms, slugs, crayfish, shrimps

involucral bract: one of several bracts that form a whorl below a flower or flower cluster

K

key: a winged fruit, usually of an ash or maple; also called a "samara"

L

larva: immature forms of an animal that differ from the adult

leaflet: a division of a compound leaf

lenticel: a slightly raised portion of bark where the cells are packed more loosely, allowing for gas exchange with the atmosphere

lobate: having each toe individually webbed

lobe: a projecting part of a leaf or flower, usually rounded

M

metabolic rate: the rate of chemical processes in an organism

metamorphosis: the developmental transformation of an animal from larval to sexually mature adult stage

midden: the pile of cone scales found on the territories of tree squirrels, usually under a favourite tree

molt: when an animal sheds old feathers, fur or skin, to replace them with new growth

montane: of mountainous regions

myccorhizal fungi: fungi that has a mutually beneficial relationship with the roots of some seed plants

N

neotropical migrant: a bird that nests in North America, but overwinters in the New World tropics

nocturnal: active primarily at night

node: a slightly enlarged section of a stem where leaves or branches originate

nutlet: a small, hard, single-seeded fruit that remains closed

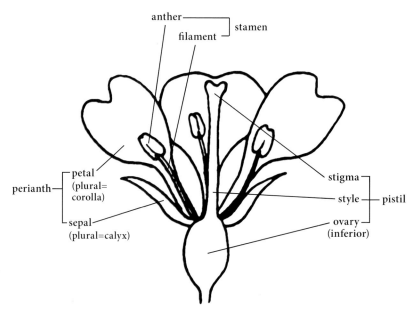

O

omnivorous: feeding on both plants and animals

ovoid: egg-shaped

P

palmate: leaflets, lobes or veins arranged around a single point, like the fingers on a hand (e.g., maple leaf)

pappus: the modified calyx of composite flowers (e.g., asters or daisies), consisting of awns, scales or bristles at the apex of the achene

parasite: a relationship between 2 species in which one benefits at the expense of the other

patagium: skin forming a flight membrane

pelage: the fur or hair of mammals

perennial: a plant that lives for several years

petal: a member of the inside ring of modified flower leaves, usually brightly coloured or white

phenology: stages of growth as influenced by climate

photosynthesis: conversion of CO_2 and water into sugars via energy of the sun

pinniped: a marine mammal with limbs that are modified to form flippers; a seal, sea-lion or walrus

pioneer species: a plant species that is capable of colonizing an otherwise unvegetated area; one of the first species to take hold in a disturbed area

piscivorous: fish-eating

pishing: a noise made to attract birds

pistil: the female organ of a flower, usually consisting of an ovary, style and stigma

plastic species: a species that can adapt to a wide range of conditions

plastron: the lower part of a turtle or tortoise shell, which covers the abdomen

poikilothermic: having a body temperature that is the same as the external environment and varies with it

pollen: the tiny grains produced in a plant's anthers and which contain the male reproductive cells

pollen cone: male cone that produces pollen

polyandry: a mating strategy in which one female mates with several males

pome: a fruit with a core, e.g., apple

precocial: animals who are active and independent at birth or hatching

prehensile: able to grasp

proboscis: the elongated tubular and flexible mouthpart of many insects

R

ray flower: in a composite flower (e.g., aster, daisy or sunflower), a type of flower usually with long, colourful petals that collectively make up the outer ring of petals (the centre of a composite flower is composed of disk flowers)

redd: spawning nest for fish

resinous: bearing resin, usually causing stickiness

rhizome: a horizontal underground stem

riparian: on the bank of a river or other watercourse

rookery: a colony of nests

runner: a slender stolon or prostrate stem that roots at the nodes or the tip

S

samara: a dry, winged fruit with usually only a single seed (e.g., maple or ash); also called a "key"

salmonid: a member of the Salmonidae family of fishes; includes trout, char, salmon, whitefish and grayling

scutes: individual plates on a turtle's shell

seed cone: female cone that produces seeds

sepal: the outer, usually green, leaf-like structures that protect the flower bud and are located at the base of an open flower

spadix: a fleshy spike with many small flowers

spathe: a leaf-like sheath that surrounds a spadix

spur: a pointed projection

stamen: the pollen-bearing organ of a flower

stigma: a receptive tip in a flower that receives pollen

stolon: a long branch or stem that runs along the ground and often propagates more plants

subnivean: below the surface of the snow

substrate: the surface that an organism grows on; the material that makes up a streambed (e.g., sand or gravel)

suckering: a method of tree and shrub reproduction in which shoots arise from an underground stem

syrinx: a bird's vocal organ

T

taproot: the main, large root of a plant from which smaller roots arise, e.g., carrot

tendril: a slender, clasping or twining outgrowth from a stem or a leaf

terrestrial: land frequenting

torpor: a state of physical inactivity

tragus: a prominent structure of the outer ear of a bat

tubercule: a round nodule or warty outgrowth

tubular flower: a type of flower in which all or some of the petals are fused together at the base

tundra: a high-altitude ecological zone at the northernmost limits of plant growth, where plants are reduced to shrubby or mat-like growth

tympanum: eardrum; the hearing organ of a frog

U

ungulate: an animal that has hooves

V

ventral: of or on the abdomen (belly)

vermiculations: wavy-patterned makings

vertebrate: an animal possessing a backbone

vibrissae: bristle-like feathers growing around the beak of birds to aid in catching insects

W

whorl: a circle of leaves or flowers around a stem

woolly: bearing long or matted hairs

REFERENCES/FURTHER READING

Acorn, John, and Ian Sheldon. 2000. *Bugs of Alberta*. Lone Pine Publishing, Edmonton, AB.

Bezener, A., and K. DeSmet. 2000. *Manitoba Birds*. Lone Pine Publishing, Edmonton, AB.

CARCNE (Canadian Amphibian and Reptile Conservation Network). Visited Nov.– Dec. 2008. Website: http://www.carcnet.ca/english/index.html

COSEWIC 2000. "COSEWIC assessment and status report on the black-footed ferret Mustela nigripes in Canada." Committee on the Status of Endangered Wildlife in Canada, Ottawa.

Elrich, P., D. Dobkin and D. Wheye 1988. *The Birder's Handbook*. Simon and Schuster/ Fireside Books, New York, NY.

Johnson, D., L. Kershaw, A. MacKinnon and J. Pojar, 1995. *Plants of the Western Boreal Forest and Aspen Parkland*. Lone Pine Publishing, Edmonton AB.

Joynt, A., and M. Sullivan. 2003. *Fish of Alberta*. Lone Pine Publishing, Edmonton AB.

Kershaw, Linda. 2003. *Saskatchewan Wayside Wildflowers*. Lone Pine Publishing, Edmonton AB.

Manitoba Wildlife. Fish and Habitat pdf series. *www.gov.mb.ca/waterstewardship/fish/index.html*

Saskatchewan Watershed Authority. "Fish Species of Saskatchewan." *www.swa.ca/Publications/Documents/FishSpeciesofSaskatchewan.pdf*

Sibley, David Allen. 2000. *National Audobon Society: The Sibley Guide to Birds of North America*. Alfred K. Knopf Inc.

Smith, Alan. 2001. *Saskatchewan*. Lone Pine Publishing, Edmonton AB.

Wilson, Don, and Sue Ruff, eds. 1999. *The Smithsonian Book of North American Mammals*. UBC Press. Vancouver and Toronto, in association with the Smithsonian Institution Press and the American Society of Mammalogists.

Vance, F.R., J.R. Jowsey, J.S. McLean and F.A. Switzer. 1999. *Wildflowers Across the Prairies*. Greystone Books, Douglas and McIntyre Publishing Group, Vancouver/ Toronto.

INDEX

Names in **boldface** type indicate primary species.

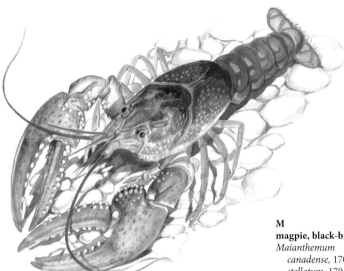

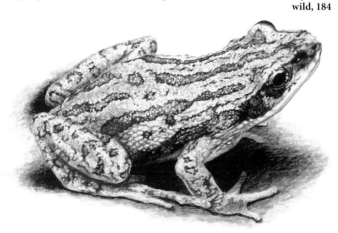

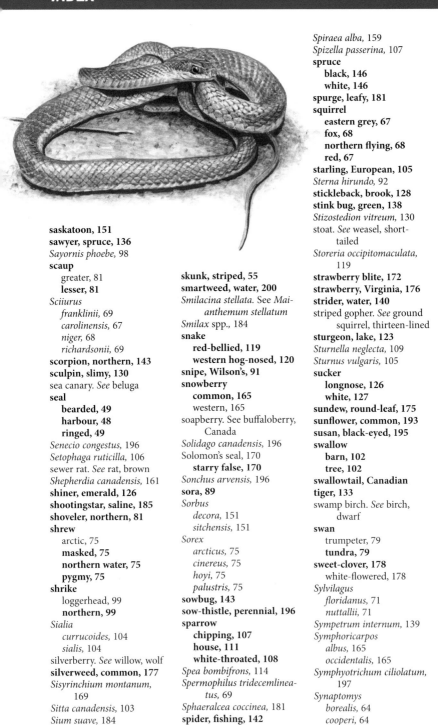

ABOUT THE AUTHOR

Krista Kagume is a passionate natural history writer who has travelled across North America, working as a freelance journalist, helicopter mechanic, deckhand on a commercial fishing boat and cycle touring guide. After earning her degree in conservation biology, Krista focused on environmental writing and consulting. She has researched tiny tundra plants, small mammals and raptors in the NWT, studied organic farming in the prairies and participated in a grizzly bear immobilization. She currently lives outside of Edmonton with her adventurous husband, three children and their organic vegetable garden.